Dear Gene,

Thank you so much for coming down this weekend to help us with the house.

Without my parents close by it is very comforting to know I have a father that can help with advice and knowledge to make our dream come true.

May God Bless you for this generous and kind act.

Mark & Michelle, Sam & Sarah.

INTELLIGENT TROUTING

fly fishing basics and beyond

Three Thousand Deluxe Copies and One Hundred Twenty-five Limited Editions of

INTELLIGENT TROUTING
fly fishing basics and beyond
have been produced by
Gilliland Printing

Printed in the United States of America
10 9 8 7 6 5 4 3 2 1

Designed by Nancy L. Chepelsky

Library of Congress Cataloging-in-Publication Data

Zacoi, Thomas Neil.
Intelligent Trouting, fly fishing basics and beyond/Thomas Neil Zacoi.
Illustrated by Jeff Wynn.
p. cm.
1. Fly fishing instruction. 2. Fly fishing anecdotes and biographies.
I. Title.
SH454.2.Z28 1999
799.1755 98-06069 CIP
ISBN 0-9664206-0-8 [pbk.]
ISBN 0-9664206-1-6 [hbk.]

This publication was made possible
in part by a grant from

T.A. Robinson

on behalf of Corey, Justin and Lindsay

Jack D. Smith, M.D.

Michael A. Tranovich, M.D.

net proceeds to benefit

Boy Scouts of America

Federation of Fly Fishers

Trout Unlimited

Intelligent Trouting

fly fishing basics and beyond

by Thomas Neil Zacoi

Illustrated by
Jeff Wynn

Introduction by
Bernard "Lefty" Kreh

Edited by
George L. Kesel
Lisa M. Pasquini
and
Malcolm Seaholm

Cover design and typography by
John Hinderliter
and
Robert Casey and Associates, Ltd.

Graphic design by
Jami F. Marlowe

Book design by
Nancy L. Chepelsky
Print-Craft Studio

Dedication And Acknowledgments

I am fortunate to have been surrounded by interesting and exciting people throughout my life. These characters are woven into the fabric of my being and have become the delight of my life. Our interactions and relationships have provided some of the material that comprises this book.

Special thanks to my friends and fellow instructors, Rich DiStanislao, Rich Roseborough and Earl Shapiro, and to Gary Borger, John Goddard, Lefty Kreh and Joan Wulff for their guidance and encouragement; to Pennsylvania State University entomologist Greg Hoover and to Jeff Wynn for his magnificent artwork and illustrations which have truly made my book beautiful.

I dedicate this work to my son Neil, my new fishing buddies, Sara and Maggie, to Fran Villella who introduced me to fly fishing and to all my friends, students and customers who give my life such purpose, challenge and enjoyment.

In addition, I must acknowledge and sincerely thank some of America's foremost angling authorities for their time and advice: George Anderson, Fred Arbona, Barry Beck, Cathy Beck, Fran Betters, Stan Bogdan, Al Caucci, Leon Chandler, George Harvey, Joe Humphreys, Ed Jaworowski, Mel Krieger, Gary LaFontaine, Mike Lawson, Maggie Merriman, Lori-Ann Murphy, Harry Murray, Robert Nastasi, Dr. Carl Richards, Tom Rosenbauer, Ernest Schwiebert, Ed Shenk, Doug Swisher, Dave Whitlock, and the late Lee Wulff. I can never repay them for their contributions–the many insightful comments you will read throughout the text.

I am indebted to Nancy Chepelsky, Daria Herrod, George L. Kesel, Lisa Pasquini, and Mac Seaholm who spent untold hours preparing this manuscript for publication. And last, but certainly not least, to Tom Robinson, Jack Smith, and Mike Tranovich. I value our friendship and appreciate your generosity and faith in me.

TABLE OF CONTENTS

Chapter Six

Chapter Seven

Chapter Eight

Chapter Nine

Chapter Ten

INTRODUCTION

Tom Zacoi has written a good book. So what can be different about another book on trout fishing? It is a little different in that it is not only filled with very useful information, but also has a bit of interesting writing about the sport and people in it.

This is not a book about steelhead, bass or saltwater fly fishing. Instead, it deals only with trout and it does that very well. The information on knots is excellent and almost every trout fisherman will benefit from reading it. The tackle chapter gives some important insights into the gear needed to land one of fly fishing's most cherished species.

The chapter on reading the water may be worth the price of the book. Absorb the information in the chapter, "Where the Trout Live," and almost every fisherman will better understand how to approach and what to present to this finicky fish.

In short, trout fishermen everywhere can benefit from the years of experience that Tom has put into these pages.

— Lefty Kreh

PREFACE

Years ago, as the tenth anniversary of the Roseborough Fly Fishing School concluded, it dawned on me that we give our students 20 years of experience in two days, yet nothing tangible to take home as a reference. To remedy this oversight, I decided to write this book.

Most fly fishing shops have shelves bulging with how-to books and tapes, the majority of which focus on some small segment of this sport. Their scope is often so narrow or so advanced that a novice may read a dozen of them and still not understand what he or she needs to know to enjoy the sport. Even worse, some authors give confusing, contradictory, inadequate or erroneous information, and the reader comes away with the misconception that fly fishing is complicated, time consuming, and outrageously expensive and then gives up before getting started.

Fifteen years of teaching the sport has given me some insight into working with beginners and triggered my desire to offer our students and the general public a compendium of essential fly fishing information. This book, along with some hands-on casting lessons from a qualified instructor and practice, will give you the basic knowledge and, I hope, the confidence to catch trout.

Each chapter of instruction is followed by a true story based on a lifetime of friends and fishing. Over the years, I've been blessed to know some extraordinary people and have had the opportunity to enjoy some unique fishing and teaching experiences. I have memories to spare, and I've included profiles of some of these unforgettable characters along with accounts of several of the adventures that we have shared. I truly hope you find them to be a pleasant diversion from the main text.

WYNN

From The Author

Standing before another new fly fishing class, I can't help but wonder what the weekend has in store for all of us. I look into my students' eyes, wide with excitement and filled with curiosity. Am I prepared to teach them how to fall in love with a sport they know nothing about in only two days?

Though it be the goal, I've often thought that maybe the worst thing that one of these beginners can do is catch a fish. After all, we live in a world that makes almost everything look easy; read a book, take a lesson and become an instant success! Perhaps the following words penned long ago better express my sentiments.

> *"Now for the art of catching fish, that is, how to make a man that was none to be an angler by a book, he that undertakes it shall undertake a harder task than Mr. Hales, that in a printed book called The Private School of Defense undertook to teach the art of fencing, and was laughed at for his labour. Not but that many useful things might be observed out of that book, but that the act was not to be taught by words; nor is the art of angling."*
>
> – *Izaak Walton*

How then can I achieve that which Father Izaak could not? All I can do is pass on, with patience and enthusiasm, that which was graciously given to me by those much wiser and instill in my students the understanding that it's truly not the catching that's important; it's the fishing!

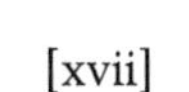

Intelligent Trouting

fly fishing basics and beyond

Chapter One

What Is A Fly Fisherman?

The fisherman made repeated fine casts without reward. He stopped periodically four times to observe the insect activity and change patterns. On the fifth choice he began to get results. While I stood and watched this expert angler, it was suddenly borne in upon me that here is a sport carried to the verge of art and well beyond the boundaries of scholarship. I saw that trout fishing might amount to a good deal more than merely 'catching a mess of fish.' It has a code, a technique, a tradition, a history. To succeed at it evidently required a good deal more than strong tackle and long patience. Here was scope for intelligence, study and skill that grows with the years.

– Odell Shephard

ly fishing was brought to America by the colonists. A recent American Fly Fishing Trade Association survey revealed that nearly eight million American men, women and children fly fish.

Those who stay with the sport go through an evolutionary process. Initially, beginners want to catch the most fish. It's a numbers game for them. Gradually, with experience, the intermediate angler desires to catch the biggest and hang it on the wall. Finally, the veteran seeks the most difficult catch, challenged by the pursuit rather than the prize.

Why Choose Fly Fishing?

Some people fly fish because they learned the sport growing up. Others because they read about it in a book, or saw the 1992 movie, *A River Runs Through It.*

In his 1964 bestseller, *Anatomy of a Fisherman,* respected author John Voelker Esq. (aka, Robert Traver), wrote the short story, "Testament of a Fisherman." This excerpt paints a unique picture that answers the question, why fish? "I fish because I love to; because I love the environs where trout are found, which are invariably beautiful, and hate the environs where crowds of people are found, which are invariably ugly; because of all the television commercials, cocktail parties, and assorted social posturing I thus escape; because, in a world where most men seem to spend their lives doing things they hate, my fishing is at once an endless source of delight and an act of small rebellion; because trout do not lie or cheat and cannot be bought or bribed

FIGURE 1.1

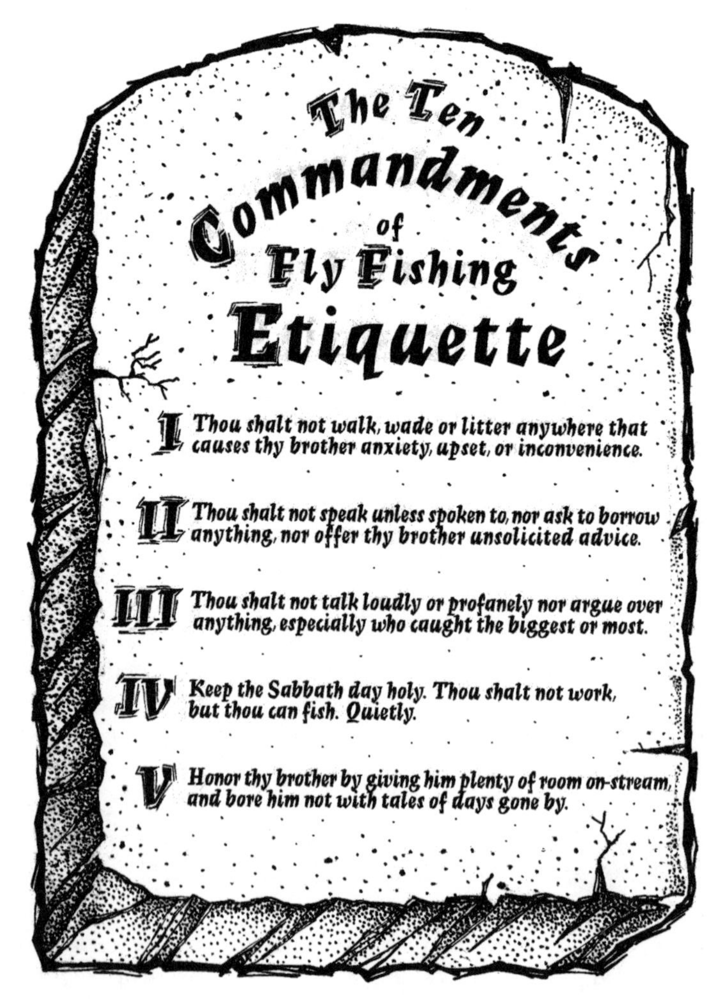

FIGURE 1.2

or impressed by power, but respond only to quietude and humility and endless patience; because I suspect that men are going along this way for the last time, and I for one don't want to waste the trip; because mercifully there are no telephones on trout waters; because only in the woods can I find solitude without loneliness; because bourbon out of an old tin cup always tastes better out there; because maybe one day I will catch a mermaid; and, fi-

FIGURE 1.3

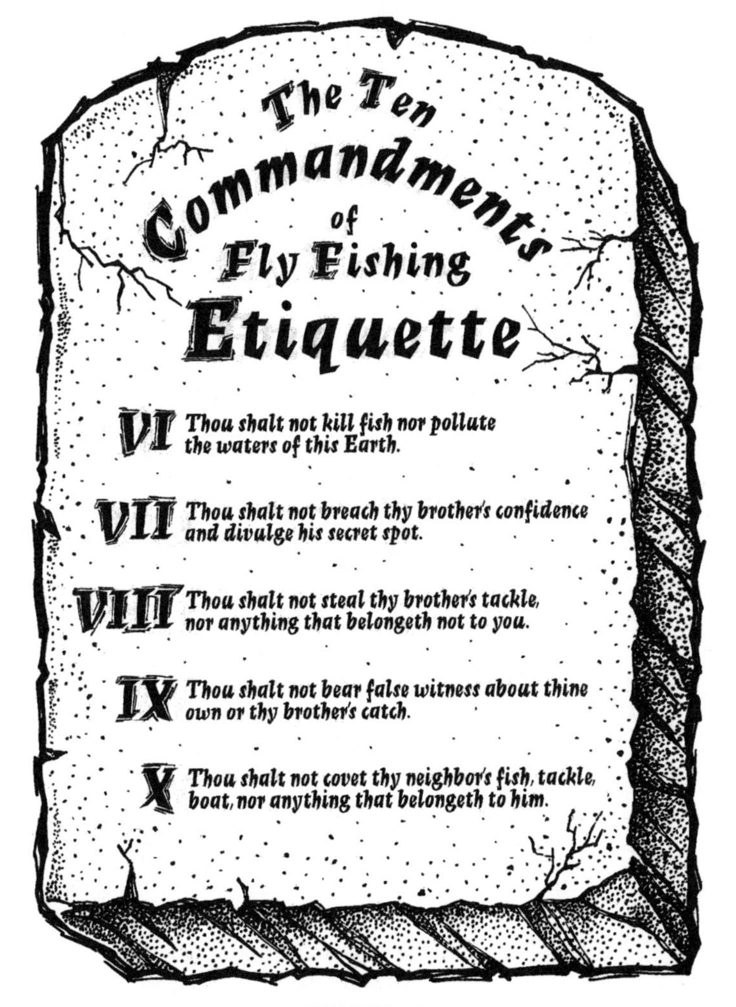

FIGURE 1.4

nally, not because I regard fishing as being so terribly important but because I suspect that so many of the other concerns of men are equally unimportant – and not nearly so much fun."

The Code Of Ethics

With a decreasing amount of public water available to accommodate all the people who participate in this sport, we need to behave properly while on stream. Author, instructor and Pennsylvania State University fly fishing Professor Emeritus George Harvey feels etiquette is one of the significant lessons to convey to everyone, beginner and veteran alike. Professor Harvey contends, "With all the overcrowding today, ethics is very important," and adds that, "the rule of conduct on the stream is to respect the rights of other fishermen." The Father of American dry-fly fishing, Theodore Gordon, recognized this problem back at the turn of the 20th century when he wrote, "The enormous increase in the number of anglers in recent years has made it necessary that all true sportsmen should consider the interests of others as well as their own."

Almost everyone is familiar with the biblical story of Moses bringing the Ten Commandments down from Mount Sinai (Figure 1.1). But what you may not be aware of is what is chiseled on the back of them (Figure 1.3). With all due respect, the "Ten Commandments of Fly Fishing Etiquette" (Figures 1.2, 1.4) are no laughing matter, and I hope you will not only take them seriously, but practice them every time you go fishing.

Courtesy Counts And Can Be Contagious

If you encounter other anglers either in the water or fishing from the bank, allow at least 100 feet of space (the approximate length of your fly line) between you and them upstream, downstream, in front and behind. This space will ensure that your shadow will not frighten the fish that your neighbor(s) may be casting to, nor will you be a distraction or an obstacle in any way.

Fly fishing is not a spectator sport or a team event. Therefore, avoid striking up a conversation while on stream. Speak only if spoken to, whether you know the person or not. A simple greeting, however, is considered sociable and tolerable. In addition, courtesy dictates that you never wade into the water or try to cross the stream in close proximity to another angler unless a dam or walkway separates the two of you. People react differently to the presence of others. Therefore, if someone gets too close to you, you may be better off to simply find another place to fish. I suggest this alternative rather than having a confrontation on stream. If, however, you have the persistence and fortitude, you can either wait until they pass by or politely request that they give you more room or ask them to leave.

As more public water becomes lost to privatization, it would be advantageous for you to introduce yourself to the property owner(s) before fishing on private property. Often, a polite request for permission to fish will gain you access to the stream. Please remember to respect their land–do not block access to driveways and fields, release the fish that you catch and thank your benefactor before you leave.

What Is A Fly Fisherman?

If you ask a dozen people, you'll undoubtedly get many different answers. Challenged by my own question, I spoke to 24 men and women who fly fish. The following is a summary of what they said:

First and foremost, the term "fly fisherman" is a misnomer. This sport attracts women and children, too. Old or young, rich or poor, physically healthy or handicapped, anyone can participate, and millions do. Fly fishermen come in all shapes and sizes and from every walk of life.

Fly fishermen prefer using artificial flies to lures or live bait. They carefully stalk the stream and enjoy the time-honored tradition of casting to trout they can see. As fly fishermen continue to refine their skills, they come to pride themselves on being imaginative, independent, observant and resourceful. Conscientious and courteous, they are always honest and follow the responsible angler's code of ethics. Fly fishermen appreciate the solitude of the sport, long to be outdoors, and relish every opportunity to go fishing, leaving the stream and its surroundings exactly as they found them–often better. Fly fishermen can delight in another angler's fishing success and aren't too disappointed if they don't catch anything at all! Fly fishermen love to teach and are willing to share their knowledge with others. They are passionate about environmental issues and give generously of their time and their money or both to help protect and preserve the sport for future generations. Last, responsible fly fishermen everywhere know that trout, specifically wild trout, are a precious and limited natural resource. Therefore, they take great pleasure in releasing unharmed most, if not all, of the fish that they catch.

AN AMERICAN CLASSIC

Old money whispers, like a Bogdan reel. Both are traditions of a similar sort - understated; understood without the need of flashy proclamations.

– John Merwin

ing! Ring! Ring!

"Hello."

"Hello, Stan."

"Who is this?"

"It's Tom Zacoi."

"Zaaaaacoi, what do *you* want?"

Oh, that Yankee humor! Believe it or not, this is how almost every conversation starts when I call to speak with the legendary reelmaker Stan Bogdan.

When I held and admired the craftsmanship of the first reel that I purchased from him, I felt I had to know more about the man who made it. After a few inquiries, I got his phone number, and we've maintained a long-distance relationship for 15 years.

I can just imagine Stan speaking to me on an old black rotary phone nailed to a wooden pillar in the dirty brick mill building where his shop is located.

He rents space from a machine-tool company in Nashua, New Hampshire. As a matter of fact, Stan told me his landlord is so bad that "five years ago, I went fishing for a week and came back to discover that my entire shop had been moved to another corner of the building." It's rumored that the orders penciled on his phone pillar are gone, victims of the owner's fresh coat of paint. I asked him if it was true.

"Well, maybe."

"Did you lose any orders?" I asked.

"A few," he conceded.

As approachable as Stan is, I've always had the impression that if he doesn't like you, you'll never get a reel from him. Of course, you can always buy one at an auction, but at a price that is often hundreds of dollars more than what Stan charges for a new reel. "If that's what people are willing to pay, it must be worth it to them," he said.

This native New Englander has been producing reels since 1940, his work interrupted only by the shortage of materials during World War II. In the four decades that followed the 40's, it was a common sentiment among fly fishermen that "no one" would pay more than twenty dollars for a reel. All this time, however, Stan has labored in relative obscurity, producing reels of uncompromising quality costing ten times that amount. During those years, Bogdan reels were distributed by Abercrombie & Fitch and Orvis. The discriminating anglers who purchased them knew fishing. They were in search of big fish and demanded a reel that simply wouldn't fail. A Bogdan reel fit their needs perfectly, and although he keeps meticulous records, Stan couldn't even hazard a guess as to how many reels he's made. He did say that "some years we only made parts, and then the next year we filled hundreds of orders."

Every inch of his 15 x 15 square-foot shop is put to good use. The dimly lit room holds two lathes, a milling machine, a drill press, and parts and pieces in boxes all over the floor. Stan is quick to point out that all the machines are pre-World War II. From start to finish, "It takes about 13 hours to finish one reel," Stan told me. He takes great pride and satisfaction in the business that he started with a meager investment of $440 and some obsolete equipment in cramped quarters.

Like his father before him, Stan became a machinist, and his son Steve now carries on the family tradition. But Stan is more than a machinist; Stanley Bogdan is an artisan. If you take a good look at the proliferation of "new reels" on the market today, virtually all of them have copied some aspect of his, including their cosmetic appearance. I asked him how he felt about that, and he said, "What are you going to do? I can't sue them. They're only copies anyway!" I got the impression that he really doesn't "give a darn."

"There's plenty of room in the marketplace for them, too," Stan allowed. Without saying so, it seemed we both acknowledged that no other reels are better than his, and most aren't nearly as good. Anyway, he can't fill all the orders he has now, so there's no sense in worrying about the others.

Stan's reels have been his entrée into the finest social circles in the fly fishing world. He has been the guest of actors, professional athletes, heads of state, politicians and the captains of industry who have purchased his reels. He has fished extensively throughout this country and abroad. Stan told me that his favorite stream is the Alta in Norway which he has visited on three occasions. He considers himself blessed to have received such recognition and attention while he's still alive, and he's thankful to have the good health necessary to do all the traveling that he does.

I asked him what he would most like to be remembered for and he said, "I'm not a 'BS' artist. I can't stand a phony. I've done everything my way, and to the best of my ability. That's all I care about."

A few years ago, a potential customer inquired if the reels came with a guarantee. Stan replied, "Yes they do, for one crank!"

Needless to say, that man never got one! Stan isn't known for his tact and diplomacy, but I can tell you firsthand that he has a great sense of humor. He is feisty and tough and can take it as well as dish it out. The late Wes Jordan, a rodmaking legend, aptly and affectionately passed on his uncle's nickname to Stan, "The Bull of the Restigouche."

But there's another side to this multi-faceted man. Underneath his seemingly brusque and sarcastic exterior lies a heart of gold. Stan donates to a variety of charities and supports any effort that benefits the Atlantic Salmon. However, his most generous act came a few years ago when Phyllis, his wife since 1944, became very ill for an extended period of time. Stan decided he would care for her at home, and along with his daughter-in-law, Sandy, and a hospice nurse, did so lovingly. Stan's commitment to his wife speaks volumes about his unselfish character.[1]

Stanley Edward Bogdan is disarmingly soft-spoken and unpretentious, an 80-year-old American classic. His reels are among the best examples of the finest tradition of reel-making craftsmanship. He never intended them to be hidden in some dusty curio cabinet. Instead, Stan makes reels to be used, and they have stood the test of time. If you're ever fortunate enough to have him make one for you, you'll be getting more than you bargained for–a piece of the man who made it.

1. Phyllis Mason Bogdan passed away October 27, 1995.

Chapter Two

Let's Gear Up

Lust for gear is widespread among American men. We think that if we have the right equipment, we will acquire expertise and that expertise will bring happiness.

– Howell Raines

Unless you are among the fortunate few who live by a quality trout stream, you will join the vast majority of us who have to travel a considerable distance to get to a good place to fish. If your favorite hot spots are anything like mine, there is no tackle dealer close by, so you will want to take everything you need with you. Unfortunately, beginners don't bring enough gear, and some of what they do bring is of little use. Having said that, I must caution you that it is better to err on the side of overpacking than to have to do without.

Anyone trying this sport for the first time does not need to buy more than a beginner's rod and reel outfit, a vest with the basic accessories, a fishing license with a trout stamp, if required, and a handful of flies. However, if you plan to attend a fly fishing school, and I hope that you will, some of the aforementioned gear may be provided for you. Therefore, there is no need to purchase a lot of tackle to get started.

In my experience most students at our weekend schools can tell early on if they like fly fishing and want to learn more about it. I developed the checklists on the following pages (Figures 2.1, 2.2) for those who are serious about continuing with this sport. These lists should be used as a general guide only. Keep in mind that what you take with you will vary according to the time of year and your personal preference. You may have much of this gear already. I have also indicated quantities in certain key categories to ensure against a ruined trip in case you lose or break one of these essentials.

The Vest

One of the most important pieces of fly fishing gear is the vest. Vests

FLY FISHING TRIP CHECKLIST

Day Trip - Essentials & Extras

ESSENTIALS

- ❒ Aspergum® & Pepto Bismol® Tablets
- ❒ Aspirin/Tylenol®
- ❒ Amadou
- ❒ Auto & Health Insurance Cards
- ❒ Canteen w/Water
- ❒ Cash/Credit Cards/Checkbook
- ❒ Clothing (Change Of)
- ❒ Driver's License & Vehicle Registration
- ❒ Drying Patch (Wool/Foam)
- ❒ Emergency Kit w/Safety Pins
- ❒ E-Z Hook Tool® X 2 ea.
- ❒ First Aid Kit
- ❒ Flex-lite® w/Batteries
- ❒ Fly Box(es) w/Flies
- ❒ Fly Floatant & Fly Dry Crystals
- ❒ Glasses (Clear Lens w/Bifocal)
- ❒ Hand Sanitizer & Paper Towels
- ❒ Hat
- ❒ Hatch Chart
- ❒ Hemostat w/Zinger
- ❒ Knife (Small Pocket)
- ❒ Lead Shot/Soft Lead
- ❒ Leader(s) & Leader Gauge
- ❒ Map/Directions
- ❒ Matches (Waterproof)
- ❒ Nail Knot Tool/Tube
- ❒ Nipper w/Needle X 2 ea. w/Zinger
- ❒ Nylon Cord & Clothes Hangers (Wire)
- ❒ Plastic Dishpan/Large Bucket
- ❒ Plastic Tall Kitchen Bags
- ❒ Pliers (Sm. Smooth Jaw) w/Zinger
- ❒ Prescription Glasses w/Lanyard
- ❒ Prescription Medications
- ❒ Raincoat w/Hood (Waterproof)
- ❒ Reels w/Lines & Backing X 2 ea.
- ❒ Rods X 2 ea.
- ❒ Signed Fishing License w/Holder
- ❒ Signed Trout Stamp w/Photo ID
- ❒ Spare Tire w/Jack
- ❒ Sunglasses (Polarized) w/Lanyard
- ❒ Tippet Material w/Dispenser
- ❒ Toilet Paper & Tucks® (Bagged)
- ❒ Tool Kit (Small) w/Duct Tape®
- ❒ Vest (Fishing) & Net w/Retriever
- ❒ Wader Repair Kit
- ❒ Waders/Hip Boots X 2 ea.
- ❒ Wet Ones® (Moist Towelettes)
- ❒ Wristwatch (Waterproof)
- ❒ Zingers X 2 ea.

❒ **EXTRAS**

- ❒ AAA Card
- ❒ Advil®/Contac®
- ❒ Bandana/Handkerchief
- ❒ Bathing Suit
- ❒ Belt(s)
- ❒ Bicycle Pump w/Needle
- ❒ Boots (Rubber/Hiking)
- ❒ Bottle/Can Opener & Corkscrew
- ❒ Camera w/Film/Flash (Bagged)
- ❒ Camera Lens Cleaner Kit
- ❒ Camera Tripod
- ❒ Canoe w/Paddles
- ❒ Cel-phone w/Battery(s)
- ❒ Cepacol®/Listerine®
- ❒ Chains (Stream Cleats)
- ❒ Chapstick® w/Sunblock
- ❒ Chewing Gum/Hard Candy
- ❒ Compass
- ❒ Cooking Equipment (Misc.)
- ❒ Cooler w/Ice or Ice Packs
- ❒ Cough Drops
- ❒ Dimetapp®/Motrin®
- ❒ Diving Goggles
- ❒ Drinking Glass(s)/Plate(s)
- ❒ Dry Duffle (Waterproof)
- ❒ Eating Utensil(s)/Pot(s) & Pan(s)
- ❒ Emergency Phone No.'s List
- ❒ Emory Cloth/Steel Wool
- ❒ Fishing Diary
- ❒ Fishing Thermometer
- ❒ Flashlight w/Batteries
- ❒ Flex-All 454®
- ❒ Flex-lite® Extra Bulb & Battery(s)
- ❒ Flies (extra) w/Boxes
- ❒ Flip Focals
- ❒ Float Tube w/Fins & Repair Kit
- ❒ Fly Tying Kit w/Material(s)
- ❒ Folding Chair/Stool/Table
- ❒ Food/Drinks/Condiments
- ❒ Glasses Lanyard(s)
- ❒ Gloves
- ❒ Gravel Guards
- ❒ Grill w/Charcoal & Lighter Fluid
- ❒ Hair Dryer
- ❒ Hand Lotion
- ❒ Hook Sharpener
- ❒ Inflatable PFD
- ❒ Insect Bite Lotion
- ❒ Insect I.D. Book
- ❒ Insect Net/Seine
- ❒ Insect Repellent
- ❒ Jumper Cables/Flares
- ❒ Knot Tying Book
- ❒ Krazy Glue®
- ❒ Long Underwear
- ❒ Magnifier (Hand Lens)
- ❒ Medical Thermometer
- ❒ Micro-Screwdriver Set
- ❒ Monocular/Binoculars
- ❒ Nail Clippers/Nail File
- ❒ Napkins (Bagged)
- ❒ 1 Drop Vinyl Adhesive®
- ❒ Papertowels (Bagged)
- ❒ Pen/Pencil w/Paper
- ❒ Portable Radio w/Batteries
- ❒ Portable Stove w/Propane Tank
- ❒ Q-tips®/Toothpicks
- ❒ Rainpants (Waterproof)
- ❒ Rolaids®/Tums®
- ❒ Rod Repair Kit
- ❒ Roof Rack
- ❒ Rubber Rod Grips X 2 ea.
- ❒ Salt Pills
- ❒ Scale (Fishing)
- ❒ Smoking/Chewing Material
- ❒ Snake Bite Kit
- ❒ Soap (Biodegradable)
- ❒ Spare Float Tube
- ❒ Strike Indicator(s)
- ❒ Sunburn Cream w/Aloe
- ❒ Sunscreen
- ❒ Sweater/Turtleneck
- ❒ Sweatshirt (Hooded)
- ❒ Swiss Army Knife®
- ❒ Tape Measure
- ❒ Thermos®
- ❒ Toilet Kit (Personal)
- ❒ Tow Rope/Bungee Cords
- ❒ Tweezers w/Zinger
- ❒ Vaseline®
- ❒ Visine® Eye Drops
- ❒ Wader Belt & Suspenders
- ❒ Wader Socks (In/Outside)
- ❒ Wading Shoes
- ❒ Wading Staff
- ❒ Whistle w/Lanyard
- ❒ Windbreaker
- ❒ Zinc Oxide
- ❒ Ziploc® Freezer Bags

This list is intended as a general guide; local conditions may dictate variations.

FIGURE 2.1

come in a variety of styles, colors, and prices. In addition, vests are sold in various sizes for men, women and children and are available in several types of material and a number of different pocket configurations. Try some on before you make your purchase. The vest will be your "home away from home." It should contain all of the items that you will need on stream that day, but don't over fill the pockets.

I have been told that some instructors actually teach their students

FLY FISHING TRIP CHECKLIST

Extended Trip - Essentials & Extras Added to the Day Trip List

- ❒ Air/Foam Mattress
- ❒ Alarm Clock
- ❒ Aluminum Foil
- ❒ Aqua Seal®
- ❒ Bath Towel
- ❒ Bird Finder I.D. Book
- ❒ Bleach
- ❒ Boat/Trailer/RV/Canoe
- ❒ Books on Tape/CD's
- ❒ Calamine Lotion
- ❒ Candles
- ❒ Clothes Line w/Hangers
- ❒ Cot (Folding)
- ❒ Dental Floss
- ❒ Dish Detergent
- ❒ Dish Supplies
- ❒ Envelopes w/Stamps
- ❒ Ferrule Cement
- ❒ Film Mailers w/Extra Film
- ❒ Flower I.D. Book
- ❒ Fly Line(s)
- ❒ Fly Line Cleaner Kit
- ❒ Garbage Bags (Plastic)
- ❒ Glass Cleaner
- ❒ Ground Cloth
- ❒ Hand Towel
- ❒ Halazone Tablets
- ❒ Hotel Confirmation No.
- ❒ Hotel Reservations
- ❒ Itinerary
- ❒ Kleenex®
- ❒ Lantern
- ❒ Line Winder
- ❒ Luggage
- ❒ Mirror
- ❒ Passport/Visa
- ❒ Plastic Wrap
- ❒ Playing Cards/Games
- ❒ Pillow
- ❒ Reading Material
- ❒ Reel Cleaning Kit
- ❒ Reel Repair Kit
- ❒ Roof Rack
- ❒ Scissors
- ❒ Sewing Kit
- ❒ Shoes/Socks
- ❒ Shoe Laces
- ❒ Sleeping Bag
- ❒ Soap Powder (Laundry)
- ❒ Talcum/Foot Powder
- ❒ Television/VCR
- ❒ Tennis Shoes
- ❒ Tent w/Directions
- ❒ Tickets (Misc.)
- ❒ Tree Finder I.D. Book
- ❒ T-Shirts
- ❒ Twist Ties
- ❒ Underwear
- ❒ Video Tape(s)
- ❒ Vitamins
- ❒ Walkman® wTapes
- ❒ Wash Cloth
- ❒ Wool Hat

This list is intended as a general guide; local conditions may dictate variations.

FIGURE 2.2

that a vest, laden with gear, will help hold you down in fast current. Although that is true, consider that you may be standing for hours while wearing it, and a fully equipped fly fishing vest can weigh as much as 15 pounds or more. That is why many of the newer models come with a padded collar and yoke that distributes that weight evenly and more comfortably across the wearer's shoulders.

You have undoubtedly seen fishermen who have so much paraphernalia dangling from their vests that they look like a cross between General George C. Patton and the national Christmas tree! As you gain experience, you will notice that the leader and flyline can get caught in the most unlikely places, and a preponderance of gadgetry lends itself to such situations. Try to minimize the number of accessories attached to the front of your vest by pinning zingers (bottle-cap sized string or wire retractors) to the inside of the front pocket flaps of the vest, out of the way, where the accessories will stay safely retracted yet easy to find. Exposed zingers and gadgets, especially metal ones, can easily scratch the finish on your fly rod, so it is important to keep them concealed if possible. Remember that chrome zingers and shiny metal accessories can reflect the sun and frighten fish. To avoid scaring the fish, use ebonized or dark, nonreflective finishes.

Don't forget to buy a fishing license and a trout stamp if required in your state. It is a good idea to record your fishing license number on the state regulations book that comes with your license. Never expect the store clerk to do it for you. If you lose your license, a duplicate can be

FLY FISHING VEST CHECKLIST

Essentials & Extras

ESSENTIALS	EXTRAS	
❒ Aspergum® & Pepto Bismol® Tablets	❒ Bandana/Handkerchief	❒ Knife (Small Pocket)
❒ Amadou/Fly Dry Crystals	❒ Binoculars/Monocular	❒ Knot Tying Book
❒ Drying Patch (Wool/Foam)	❒ Camera w/Film/Flash (Bagged)	❒ Leader(s)
❒ Emergency Kit & First Aid Kit	❒ Canteen w/Water	❒ Leader Gauge
❒ E-Z Hook Tool® X 2 ea.	❒ Chapstick® w/Sunblock	❒ Magnifier (Hand Lens)
❒ Flex-lite® w/Batteries	❒ Chewing Gum	❒ Matches (Waterproof)
❒ Fly Box(es) w/ Flies	❒ Chewing Material	❒ Nail Knot Tool/Tube
❒ Fly Floatant & Lead Shot/Soft Lead	❒ Fishing thermometer	❒ 1 Drop Vinyl Adhesive®
❒ Hemostat w/Zinger	❒ Flip Focals	❒ Pen/Pencil w/Paper
❒ Nipper w/Needle x 2 ea. w/Zinger	❒ Food (Bagged)	❒ Raincoat w/Hood (Waterproof)
❒ Pliers (Small Smooth Jaw) w/Zinger	❒ Glasses (Clear Lens w/Lanyard)	❒ Scale (Fishing)
❒ Prescription Glasses w/Lanyard	❒ Glasses Lanyard(s)	❒ Smoking Material
❒ Prescription Medications w/Tucks®	❒ Hard Candy	❒ Strike Indicator(s)
❒ Signed Fishing License w/Holder	❒ Hatch Chart	❒ Sunscreen
❒ Signed Trout Stamp w/Photo ID	❒ Hook Sharpener	❒ Tape Measure
❒ Sunglasses (Polarized) w/Lanyard	❒ Inflatable PFD	❒ Toiletries (Personal)
❒ Tippet Material w/Dispenser	❒ Insect ID Book	❒ Tweezers w/Zinger
❒ Toilet Paper w/Wet Ones® (Bagged)	❒ Insect Net/Seine	❒ Wader Repair Kit
❒ Vest (Fishing) & Net w/Retriever	❒ Insect Repellent	❒ Whistle w/Lanyard
		❒ Zinger (extra)

This list is intended as a general guide; local conditions may dictate variations.

FIGURE 2.3

more easily obtained when you have this information available. You might also want to save your old photo driver's license and tuck it in the holder behind your fishing license. Many states require licensed fishermen to carry photo identification at all times.

The accompanying checklist (Figure 2.3) is a general guide to the essentials and extras that you may need, or want, to have in your vest. Until you gain experience and develop your personal preferences, avoid indiscriminate purchases, especially from a catalog, which could result in acquiring unnecessary, expensive, or poor quality merchandise.

Many of the following accessories can be conveniently stored in the pockets in front, in back or inside the vest. I consider all of them essential and suggest they be "standard issue" for everyone.

1. Drying patch, signed fishing license, trout stamp, photo identification. If you put your flies away while they are still wet, the hooks can rust. In addition, you run the risk of mold destroying the fly dressings or the hackles remaining dirty and matted. A wool or foam patch attached to the front of your vest will hold the flies securely while they air dry. Barbless flies can be safely stored in a small plastic fly box or an empty 35mm film container fastened to the front of your vest. Both should be perforated to allow air to circulate and dry the hooks and material. The Fly Trap®, a new product manufactured by Water Works of Ketchum, Idaho, is designed specifically for this purpose.

A current, signed fishing license, trout stamp, and photo identification are essential. In most states they must be displayed while on stream which necessitates the use of a clear plastic pin-on holder. You can cover and protect your license in plastic wrap, a Ziploc® bag or a moisture proof, press-top-seal plastic pin-on holder. In many states residents under 16 years of age fish for free. However, regulations vary regarding children fishing out of state. Therefore, it's a good idea to call ahead before leaving home.

2. Amadou, fly dry crystals. Amadou, imported from Europe into America, is a useful material available from many companies. It is a tree fungus found in the Black Forest of Germany that is washed, dried and sliced into round wafers. Two wafers are then glued onto a leather pad about the size of a half dollar. It looks like a castanet when closed. When a wet fly is squeezed between the wafers, Amadou acts as a super chamois for drying a fly for immediate re-use. A similar new product would be any of the crystal desiccants like Fly Drying Beads® or Shake 'N Float®. They are available in small plastic jars and, like Amadou, remove most of the moisture and slimy fish mucus from flies. Fly dry crystals go a step further in that some of them simultaneously add floatant to the fly.

3. Flex-lite®, batteries. If you fish at night, a Flex-lite® or flashlight is indispensable when changing flies, tying knots and walking in the dark. I recommend that you turn your back to the stream when using a light to tie a knot or change a fly to keep the light from reflecting off the water and possibly scaring away the very fish you are trying to catch.

4. E-Z Mini Hook® Tool, flies, boxes. Obviously, you will need an assortment of flies and something to store them in. More information on these selections can be found later in this chapter. An E-Z Mini Hook® Tool is helpful in grasping any size fly from your box and holding it securely while tying it onto your leader. A picture and description of this item can be found in Chapter Three, "Fly Lines, Terminal Tackle and Knots".

5. Floatant, lead shot/soft lead, hemostat. Don't forget floatant to help dry flies float higher and longer on top of the water; soft lead, to sink wet patterns faster when fishing below the surface; and a hemostat to facilitate hook removal from all the fish you are going to release.

6. Tippet material, dispenser. Tippet material (from 2X to 7X), preferably wound onto a round dispenser, is a necessity. It is used to extend the leader when the original leader or tippet becomes too short.

7. Nipper with needle. You will need a nipper with needle (a small sharp metal clipper) to cut tippet material and poke open a cement-clogged hook eye.

8. Pliers, zingers. Small, smooth-jaw pliers are useful for bending hook barbs. You will also need three zingers to keep the pliers, the hemostat and the nipper with needle attached to your vest and conveniently retracted.

9. Net, retractor. A net with a black 48-inch Key-Bac® retractor clipped to the D ring on the back or side of your vest will remain out of the way until it is needed to help land a large fish. The Orvis® magnetic net holder works well on small nets, and Brodin's brass snap is ideal for large nets like those used in Western and steelhead fishing.

Modern, tightly woven net bags, made from soft-stretch nylon, are less abrasive to the fish's scales. In addition, the new shallow bags don't snag in the gills as readily nor split the fins as often as the older models made from hard nylon.

10. Emergency/first aid kit. It is a good idea to have an emergency kit stashed away somewhere in your vest. Mine contains a nail knot tube (a hollow plastic Q-tip®), leaders, leader gauge, extra nipper with needle, a spare E-Z Mini Hook® Tool, Aspergum® and Pepto Bismol® tablets. You may want to customize your kit to include lip balm, sunscreen, matches or lighter, a knot-tying book, tiptop and ferrule cement, needle and thread, antiseptic and Band-Aid® adhesive strips, safety pins, or other useful items of your choice.

11. Prescription glasses, polarized sunglasses, medications. Don't forget your prescription medications and eyeglasses with lanyard.

12. Toilet paper, Tucks®, Wet-Ones®. Last, but not least, Tucks® and a packaged moist towelette similar to Wet-Ones® and some toilet paper rolled and sealed in a Ziploc® freezer bag can be a godsend.

I recommend emptying your vest at the end of the year, having it dry cleaned, and then replenishing your fly boxes and reorganizing the accessories in preparation for next season.

EYE PROTECTION

A good pair of polarized sunglasses with a lanyard and a wide-brimmed hat with a dark colored underbrim are indispensable eye protection. I suggest that you purchase a quality pair of polarized sunglasses, preferably ones with side shields. The wrap styles are ideal. The polarized lenses cut down on glare, enabling you to look deeper into the water and making it easier to see the fish and your footing while wading. Polarized sunglasses protect you from ultraviolet sunlight and the ever-present danger of getting a hook caught in your eye. In addition, factory-ground magnifying bifocals, if needed, will prove to be invaluable for the close work of tying knots and flies onto your leader. Plastic, self-adhesive magnifying bifocals are available from a number of companies and are an inexpensive alternative.

The choice in sunglasses has traditionally been a matter of personal preference. Unfortunately, in years past, little interest and even less information was available. Consequently, there weren't many options to choose from. Today, I have seen a technological revolution in eyewear that tends to fall into two general categories of interest to fly fishermen. CR-39, a hard resin polymer, and polycarbonate plastic lenses have become popular recently because they are lightweight and less expensive to manufacture than glass. Unfortunately, like plastic clip-ons, it is slightly more difficult to achieve faultless clarity and polarization with these materials. Anglers who want the best in visual acuity always choose glass. Although heavier and more costly to produce, glass lenses offer superior scratch resistance and distortion-free polarization. Both glass and plastic transition lenses can have photochromatic (light sensitive darkening) capability and come in basic brown and gray colors. In regard to lens color, experts agree that brown and amber offer exceptional UV protection, good depth perception and fine color contrast for use in fresh water fishing. Medium to dark gray tints allow for excellent UV protection while maintaining true color transmission. They are the best choice for those with sensitive eyes, and they do a superb job of cutting the harsh glare if you are saltwater fishing at the ocean.

Regardless of the lens material and color you choose, sunglasses should always be optically correct for your vision, including bifocals if needed. Anything less can cause headaches and eye strain and it will be more difficult to tie knots and accurately see the fish. A quick look at any fly fishing catalog will convince you that making a trip to your local tackle dealer or optician is an intelligent thing to do. The opportunity to try on the wide variety of frames, as well as discuss any prescription needs you may have, will be invaluable regarding this important purchase. Remember, you only have one pair of eyes, so it just makes good sense to protect them!

I encourage everyone to wear a pair of clear lens glasses with a lanyard and a magnifying bifocal, if needed, for early morning, late evening and night use. A number of companies now sell glasses for these specific purposes. Clear lens glasses offer eye protection from branches and errant casts, and in my opinion, should be worn every time you fish or walk in the dark.

It is important to keep both your sunglasses and clear lens glasses in crush proof, hardshell cases. These cases ensure that if your glasses get dropped or stepped on, the lenses are protected and the frames will not lose their face form.

Finally, I offer one last bit of advice from professional photographers Barry and Cathy Beck: "A better picture will always result if the angler removes his or her sunglasses before being photographed."

RODS, REELS AND OUTFITS

At the outset, I must tell you that the fly size you will be using and the width of the stream you are going to visit will help determine the optimal line weight you should use. I have expanded on this critical subject separately in Chapter Three, "Fly Lines, Terminal Tackle and Knots." Once you make those decisions, your choice of a rod and reel combination will be made easier.

Graphite fly rods are perfect for beginners and come in a variety of lengths, line weights and "actions" from a dozen or so manufacturers. Action refers to the profile of a flexed rod but has no bearing on your ability to catch fish. A soft rod flexes most in the lower third near the grip. Progressive action rods flex in the middle, while stiff rods flex close to the tip. This general explanation does not mean that any one action is better than another. However, it does call attention to the fact that choosing a rod is a matter of personal preference. Rods made by different manufacturers may share identical dimensions such as length and weight but will not cast or feel the same. By simply adding or subtracting one fly line weight from the rodmaker's recommendation, the action can be dramatically changed. Therefore, it is important for everyone, but especially a beginner, to be an informed and intelligent consumer and try out a variety of rods from several manufacturers.

Notwithstanding minor differences, fly rods have similar components (Figure 2.4) and tend to fall into three primary categories: lightweight, midweight and heavy duty.

Generally speaking, lightweight rods (3 and 4 weight) in 6-8 feet lengths work well in narrow streams of approximately ten yards in width, where short casts of 30 to 40 feet, smaller fly sizes (12-28) and delicate

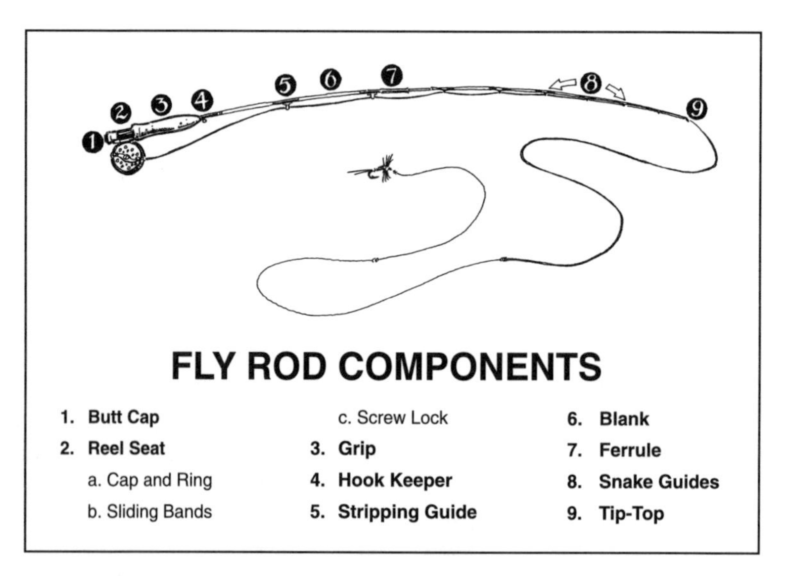

FIGURE 2.4

presentations are needed. I consider midweight rods (5-7 weight) in 7-9 feet lengths perfect for beginners. These rods can be used in all streams, small rivers and ponds and work best with flies ranging in sizes from (2-28) and where casts of 50 to 60 feet in length are required. Heavy duty rods, (8 weight and heavier) in 8 -10 feet lengths are optimally designed for use in large rivers, ponds and in saltwater fishing. They have the power necessary to cast 75 feet of line with ease and deliver the largest flies in your box. Please keep in mind that the aforementioned rod length and line weight combinations are a general guide, and no rod, regardless of price or manufacturer, can make up for a lack of casting ability.

Contemporary reels do more than simply "hold the fly line," and they, too, are divided into the same three categories of lightweight, midweight and heavy duty.

Lightweight reels are traditionally made of aluminum and are capable of handling fish measuring up to 20 inches in length and weighing up to 4 pounds. These reels are typically single action which means that for every revolution of the handle the reel spool turns once. Lightweight reels are usually designed to hold up to a 4 weight line and backing, and are used with flies ranging in sizes from 12-28. They are relatively small and will have some factory set drag that helps protect fine tippets. Midweight reels are the "work horses" of fly fishing and are a good all around choice for anyone just starting out. They, too, are traditionally single action and will accommodate fly lines and backing from 4-6 weight and flies ranging in size from 2-28. These reels often have built-in drag that helps prevent spool overrun and the resulting fly line backlash. You can purchase models with an adjustable drag system that is made to slow down larger fish like big trout and bass. Reels with adjustable drag systems are frequently manufactured with improved gears that run smoother and minimize the risk of a bigger fish breaking off. Heavy duty reels have line capacities of 6 weight and higher and hold up to 100 yards of backing or more. They are ordinarily single action but come equipped with adjustable drag systems capable of stopping game fish like salmon, steelhead and tarpon. Some high-priced models are made from brass, but most are either machined anodized aluminum or cast with a baked on finish to help prevent corrosion from saltwater.

There are two additional groups of reels that I only want to mention: Multiplier and antireverse reels have special functions, while antique and classic reels make up the collectible category. All of these reels have useful applications if they work, but none is of much value to a beginner fly fisherman because they're not designed for trout fishing or expensive.

Today's reels are extremely durable, and with routine maintenance and reasonable care should last a lifetime. This maintenance must include periodically lubricating, cleaning and drying the side plates as well as the fly line after each use. I suggest placing a silica gel capsule or packet into a fleece or foam lined reel case. The desiccant will absorb moisture and help prevent rust and mildew. All of your reels should be kept organized and protected in a kit bag. This carryall normally is made large enough to conveniently store most of your reels and fly line cleaning supplies. In addition, you may also be able to keep spare fly lines, leaders, spools of tippet material as well as reel repair tools, your camera and extra film containers in the kit bag too.

The rod and reel you choose should complement one another and be balanced (Figure 2.5). America's ambassador of fly fishing, Leon Chandler, advises, "It is important to use balanced equipment purchased from a knowledgeable retailer." Manufacturers clearly mark the optimum line weight on their rods and sometimes on the reels, too. If you have any questions about line weight, simply refer to the manufacturer's catalog for that information. If you select a 6-weight rod, for example, you should choose a 6-weight fly line and a reel to complement it. You can further tell if a rod and reel are matched by balancing the rod with the reel attached, on your finger tip, a few inches in front of the grip. If the rod doesn't tilt dramatically in either direction, the outfit is reasonably balanced.

BALANCED FLY ROD and REEL OUTFITS

Including Recommended Flies and Sizes

FISH SPECIES	***LINE WEIGHTS***	***REEL SIZES***	***ROD LENGTHS***	***FLY SIZES***
Small Trout	3 wt.– 4 wt.	Light Weight	6 feet– 8 feet	12– 28
Trout & Bass	4 wt.– 8 wt.	Mid Weight	7 feet– 9 1/2 feet	2–28 & Bassbugs
Salmon & Steelhead	6 wt.– 10 wt.	Mid & Heavy	8 1/2 feet– 10 feet	Salmon & Steelhead
Bone Fish & Permit	7 wt.– 10 wt.	Heavy Duty	8 1/2 feet– 10 feet	Saltwater Patterns
Tarpon & Ocean Fish	8 wt.– 12 wt.	Heavy Duty	8 1/2 feet– 10 feet	Saltwater Patterns

THIS CHART IS A GENERAL GUIDE ONLY

FIGURE 2.5

The stream you plan to visit, as well as the species of fish you want to catch, will help determine the optimal rod, reel and fly line you should use. This combination can be further influenced by the weather, time of year, stream conditions, length of the manufacturers product warranties and the individual temperament of the angler. In other words, there are a lot of variables that must be considered before purchasing a rod and reel, including aesthetics and personal preference. However, don't let anyone kid you: good tackle is an investment, and until you are absolutely certain that you are interested in this sport, don't rush out and purchase the first thing you see. Take your time, look around and do your homework. For example, you may find a closeout, special promotion or a salesmen's sample that has been marked down. Many companies now offer quality, balanced outfits that include a rod, reel, backing, fly line and leader. These packages are ideal for beginners because they are self-contained, factory balanced and reasonably priced.

Regardless of what you choose, never buy a rod or reel sight unseen from a catalog, especially if it's your first outfit. Internationally recognized instructor, author and casting champion Joan Wulff advises, "Never buy a rod that you haven't cast." As a courtesy to their customers, most dealers will allow you to demo their equipment prior to making a purchase.

Your local fly shop is a great place to see the wide variety of rods and reels available today. Most shop owners are qualified to assist you with your purchase and can recommend a manufacturer whose equipment is best suited to your individual needs. For example, he or she will show you the wide selection of cork grips (Figure 2.6) that come in four traditional styles: half wells, full wells, western, and cigar. Try them out and choose the one that feels most comfortable. In addition, reel seats are available in three basic variations: slide band, uplocking or downlocking. This decision, as well as your choice of a grip style, is a matter of personal preference and has little to do with performance. Your local shop owner is the factory authorized dealer for the equipment that he or she sells and can handle any problems you may have in regard to product warranties and repair work. When you outgrow your original purchases, your local fly shop is an excellent place to either trade in or resell your used tackle.

CARE FOR YOUR EQUIPMENT

I cannot tell you how many times customers have returned broken rods and reels to fly fishing shops giving every reason imaginable for the damage. Frankly, shopowners know that more often than not it is due to the customers, carelessness. For example, a few people have confessed to picking up the assembled rod by the tip, only to have it break off in

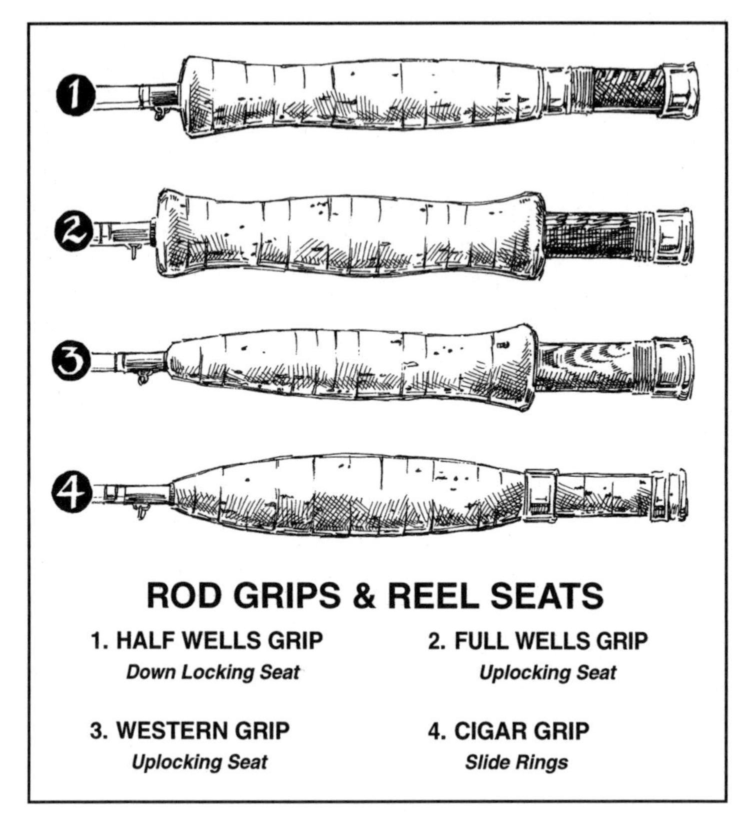

FIGURE 2.4

their hand. Another man told me he couldn't get his rod apart, so he clamped it into a vise and pulled it apart with a pair of pliers. I've often thought that the lifetime guarantees offered by many rod manufacturers contribute to some people's irresponsibility.

Ms. Heidi Lott, repair department supervisor for the R. L. Winston Rod Company cautions, "Never put a rod or rod bag away wet. I have opened rod tubes and literally poured water out of the ferrules. Once the cap is tightened, the rubber gasket seals the tube so air cannot circulate. Consequently, the moisture trapped inside can discolor, bubble or cause the varnish to peel. The reel seat can swell so much that it either cracks or becomes warped to the point that you can't even get a reel on it."

I cannot stress the importance of having a routine for taking care of your tackle. For example, store your rod in the same place when it is not in use. The first thing you should do after a day on stream is wipe your rod with a clean, damp cloth, dry it thoroughly and return the fly rod to its storage sack and tube. Screw on the tube cap and then put it back in your vehicle. This regimen ensures that the rod will not be inadvertently left on the roof, stepped on, or forgotten. It's also a good idea to drop a silica gel packet or two into the bottom of all your rod tubes. You have an investment in this sport, and it just makes good sense to protect your valuable equipment. Inscribing your name, address, and phone number on your rod tubes and all your tackle is an intelligent thing to do, too.

Everyone should carry a hand towel, handkerchief, or bandana. Holding a fish leaves your hands slimy and wet, and rather than wiping your dirty hands in the grass or on your waders, use the towel. Keeping your hands clean will also keep your cork rod grip from getting unnecessarily soiled.

Wading boots can be hung upside down to air dry. Your vest and any other wet articles should be stored indoors. Remember to clean your fly line with a cleaner/dressing after a day on stream to remove dirt, add floatability and increase performance. A clean line is easier to cast, strip in and pick up. A dirty fly line can score the inner surface of the rod guides causing the guides and the fly line to wear prematurely.

FLY BOXES

The initial selection, purchase, and organization of your fly boxes is as individual a preference as what you choose to keep in your vest. However, as you have already learned in this chapter, never indiscriminately purchase anything sight unseen from a catalog, flies and fly boxes included! I counted over four dozen different box styles, as well as hundreds of fly patterns in one catalog alone. How can a beginner know what to choose from such an extensive selection? The answer is found in chapter five, "Entomology". In addition, you can always ask someone with experience to help you or visit your local fly tackle dealer. If you're just starting out, there are excellent stream guides and hatch charts available that will indicate the appropriate patterns and fly sizes that match the time of year and specific water you are going to visit. Acquainting yourself with these resources will provide valuable information that will help you make the proper selections when you're at the shop or on the stream.

Fly boxes vary dramatically in size, inner configuration, and outer material. Although I mentioned earlier in this chapter that the fishing vest is your home away from home, I remind you again that you may be standing all day while wearing it. Therefore, it just makes good sense to choose fly boxes that are lightweight. All the major fly box manufacturers supply products that are functional and durable, and are constructed of materials that will float if the closed box is dropped in water. The other significant considerations are overall dimensions, number and size of compartments, weight and price. Fly boxes are constructed from a variety of materials including wood, aluminum, plastic, and the newest innovation, closed cell foam.

Wooden fly boxes float well and are aesthetically pleasing. However, they are usually expensive and tend to be quite heavy.

The technically advanced and superbly crafted plastic flip compartments of the Richard Wheatley Company aluminum fly boxes are a pleasure to use, but bear in mind that moving parts have a high potential for breakage. If you put more than one pattern or size in an individual compartment, it may be difficult to find and remove the fly you want to use when you are on stream. The Wheatley company does offer boxes with variations of ripple foam or flat foam sheets that eliminate the potential problems associated with their traditional flip lid boxes. Unfortunately, this import from the United Kingdom tends to be expensive and, though lighter in weight than its wooden counterpart, is also inclined to be somewhat heavy.

Plastic fly boxes eliminate most of the problems associated with the wooden and aluminum models. They are available in the widest variety of sizes and inner compartment configurations and include flat foam sheets or ripple foam that separate and elevate the flies. The ripple foam keeps the fly hackles from getting smashed when the lid is closed. You can see each individual fly, so selecting one especially while you are fishing is made easier. Most plastic boxes will float even if dropped in the water while open. They are durable, inexpensive, and are extremely lightweight.

The newest fly boxes on the market are the closed cell foam versions with a magnetic closure. This new product shares most of the advantages of the plastic models, but, at present, they are not available in a wide variety of sizes and compartmental configurations. Foam fly boxes are inexpensive, they "float like a cork," and are "light as a feather."

FLY SELECTION

A quick glance at any fly fishing catalog will convince you that your initial fly selection and purchase is best shared with someone who has some experience. I counted 187 individual fly patterns available in 556 sizes in one catalog alone.

I'll never forget my first fly-buying experience. My friend Fran Villella took me to a fly wholesaler in Penfield, Pennsylvania. When we walked into the warehouse, I was overwhelmed by the inventory. There were literally tens of thousands of boxes. Unfortunately, I still have some of the flies I bought on that visit years ago. It is too easy to get hooked as you stand in front of the display cases and look at all the flies. Do yourself a favor and go fly shopping with an experienced angler. Study a hatch chart and ask for help at the shop if you still have questions.

I own a lot of fly boxes; however, I only maintain five that I use during the season. The first box has my mayfly selection; I carry caddisfly patterns in the second; the third one holds my terrestrial ties; the fourth contains midges, and the fifth box houses all the forage fish imitations, attractor patterns and specialty items. Set up your boxes according to the system that works best for you. However, to save time on stream, you should know where each box is in your vest. It's a good idea to purchase and have at least three each of the most popular patterns in their commonly used sizes and two each of all the others. When you are fishing a long way from home, you should always bring additional flies as backups. They can be variations of the flies you already have, totally different patterns, or extras of the patterns you are using. Simply leave them in your car, and if you run out, they will be there in reserve. Don't forget to bring your fly tying kit. Having it along can save the day, especially if you don't have the pattern you need or the weather turns bad and you need something to do.

FLY CARE

The very first thing the students learn during the knot tying section of the school is to bend down the barb if their hook has one. I ask them to raise their right hand and solemnly swear to do it. We repeat this phrase in unison, and after three or four repetitions everyone starts to laugh. It bears repeating, however, because of the importance of maintaining safety. As a final step, I encourage them to get into the habit of testing and sharpening the hook point, if necessary.

Checking the hook periodically while you are fishing is a smart thing to do, especially if you've caught a fish or snagged the fly. It may sound hard to believe, but more than one angler, yours truly included, has continued to fish with a broken hook or with no fly attached at all! The chances of this happening are greater when fishing with small flies, or late at night. In addition, unsnagging a fly can dull the point and open the hook gap. Catching a fish also tends to saturate the fly with fish mucus. All of these situations demand attention and some remedial action–like sharpening the hook point, drying the fly with amadou, reapplying floatant or changing the pattern.

After your day on stream, you can either transfer the used flies to their appropriate box, or hang your vest indoors for the evening and return the flies the following morning. Keep your fly boxes organized to save valuable time on stream when you are searching to find the right pattern. If you accidentally drop your fly box into the water, either place the entire box with the lid open on the dashboard of your car or on a window sill where it can dry out in the sunshine. You can use a hair dryer to blow dry the box and the flies. If the sun is not shining, remove all the flies and turn the box upside down to dry out.

WADERS AND BOOTS

A good pair of fishing boots is essential for everyone, but especially for a beginner. Boots come in two basic styles, hip boots or chest waders, and are manufactured in four different materials: rubber, vinyl, Gore-Tex® and neoprene. Hip boots come to the top of your thighs and have straps that circle your belt to hold them up. Chest waders come to the top of your chest and have shoulder straps to hold them up. Both are available in a variety of sizes and prices and come in either boot foot or stocking foot models. As the name implies, boot foot styles have an integral boot that is permanently attached to the bottom of the wader. Stocking foot designs have a plain foot bed that require wearing a separate pair of wading shoes that are usually fitted one size larger than your street shoes.

When purchasing boots, consider a comfortable fit, where and how you plan on fishing, and last but not least, price.

If you're going to fish from the bank, hip boots are a good choice. In warm weather, a pair of lightweight nylon hip boots or chest waders may prove to be more comfortable. These products come in boot foot or stocking foot models. In the latter case, separate wading shoes are required. Waders and wading shoe sizes vary according to the manufacturer; therefore, the best advice I can give you is to never buy them from a catalog. Take a trip to your local fly fishing shop. The information that you will get in regard to the products and their warranties, as well as the opportunity to try them on, will prove to be invaluable in regard to this purchase.

If you plan on wading, especially in cold weather, I suggest neoprene or heavy vinyl chest waders. You may want to wear them with long underwear, or at least consider the new polypropylene or Thorlo® wader socks worn with the nylon chest waders. Neoprene is the overwhelming choice for cold weather fishing.

If you buy wading shoes that are constructed with a leather toe and heel protector, you should treat the leather periodically with Neatsfoot oil. This will keep the leather supple and help prevent cracking. It is also advisable to use shoe trees inside your wading shoes to keep them from shrinking and curling up at the toes.

To determine if the waders fit correctly, put them on and bend, squat, kneel and climb stairs. These movements will tell you if the fit is right. You will also want to purchase gravel guards that help minimize the amount of debris that can get into your wading shoes. Unfortunately, gravel guards are easy to lose or forget, so keep them attached around the ankles of your empty waders, or roll and store them inside your wading shoes or wader bag. Using a wader bag after fishing is a convenient way to store, organize and carry your waders, elastic wader belt, wading shoes, shoetrees, socks, gravel guards and wader repair kit. Wader bags are usually constructed with mesh panels to facilitate drying wet items.

Clothes and Weather

Keep in mind that whether your trip is one day or one week, it is important to bring plenty of clothing that is appropriate to the season. Not only do weather conditions change without warning, you never know when you might fall in the stream! It's a good idea to be prepared. Your clothing should include a pair of long underwear, a sweater, waterproof rain suit, hat and a bath towel for emergency use. Fly shops stock most of these items, but an Army & Navy surplus store can be an excellent place to purchase quality foul weather gear at reasonable prices. If your fishing plans call for out-of-town travel, phone the National Weather Service, watch the Weather Channel on cable television, log on to the Internet at http://www.weather.com or look at the weather map in your local newspaper or USA Today. An additional source for up-to-the-minute information is, American Weather Concepts (AWC) at http://www.weatherconcepts.com.

Children Have Special Needs

Fly fishing is rapidly becoming a popular family sport because everyone can participate. Recognizing this fact, a few companies now offer a limited selection of tackle that addresses children's individual needs. Please don't make a common mistake and expect your son or daughter to use your hand-me-down tackle. Cortland and Scientific Anglers have put together youth fly fishing outfits that include an 8-foot, 6-weight rod fitted with a smaller diameter grip, a matching reel, fly line, backing, leader and video tape. Kids adjust to almost anything you give them and are usually happy just to be taken along, but if you are truly serious about involving your child in this sport, you need to read *First Cast, Teaching Kids to Fly Fish* by Phil Genova, and *Fly Fishing with Children* by Philip Brunquell, M.D. According to Doctor Brunquell, the psychology of working with kids is more important than the equipment you put in their hands, and both adult and child will benefit equally. Casting expert and fishing authority, Lefty Kreh has produced an excellent video called "Flycasting with Lefty Kreh" by Gary Borger Enterprises. I suggest that you rent and watch it with your kids. If they have any questions that you cannot answer, give your local fly shop owner a call.

Children need a minimal amount of equipment, and unless you've seen it, little equals the excitement on a child's face when they open up a gift and discover a fly rod, reel, fishing vest or other tackle inside. If they're not elated, perhaps they're too young. In addition to the vest, kids need a fly box with a dozen or so flies, all with the barbs bent down, a hat, nipper with needle and zinger, a spool of 3X tippet material, net with a retractor and a pair of polarized glasses and clear lens glasses with lanyards.

Safety, in my opinion, is the most important concern when taking your children on stream. Hip boots and chest waders for children are useful and available now from a few companies, but never allow a child to go into water that is deeper than their knees. The best advice I can give is when your youngster is in the water, you should be close by watching your child, not fishing! When a group of children are fishing together it is imperative that they have adult supervision. Above all, maintain safety and make sure they are having fun. Don't forget to bring a camera and film. Give him or her lots of encouragement and don't overwhelm with too much information. Last, pack a blanket, plenty of toys, games, books, snacks and drinks to keep your kids occupied when their interest wanes. If they are old enough and your car is close by, give them a spare key.

THE LADY ANGLER

Women have unique clothing and tackle requirements, yet most manufacturers haven't appreciated the market potential that they represent. According to government research, women entering the military have approximately 55 percent less strength than men. Consequently, asking a woman to use a heavy outdated rod and reel or simply scaling down men's sizes is not the answer. As a result, you won't find a wide variety of quality tackle and accessories designed for women.

In 1996, I had the opportunity to spend some time with Joan Wulff. She explained that "a good rod with a grip proportioned for a smaller hand in a suitable length and line weight is the most important piece of tackle a woman will own." Women's rods should ideally weigh less than 3 ounces and be 8 to 9 feet long. For this reason Joan Wulff has two dozen different rods set up for the female students to try at her school.[2]

The Winston Rod Company now offers the Joan Wulff model and Orvis® makes the Mary Marbury outfit. Either one is an excellent choice.

According to industry statistics, women make up 20 percent of the fly fishing population. If you are interested in fly fishing from a woman's perspective, you must read *Joan Wulff's Fly Fishing.* There are two Web sites available for the lady angler: (1) the address for the Federation of Fly Fishers is http://www.fedflyfishers.org; go to the club house page, then click on the women's fly fishing section; (2) the new International Festival of Women Fly Fishers Web site is at http://www.fly-fishing-women.com In addition, the November/December 1997 issue of the *American Angler Magazine* lists 34 organizations for fly-fishing women.

2. The Wulff Fly Fishing School is located in the Catskill Mountains, near Roscoe, New York. It lasts three days and is scheduled every weekend in May and June except Memorial Day. Further information can be obtained by phoning, (914) 439-4060 from 9 am until 5 pm Monday through Friday.

SOME PARTING ADVICE

There are a few helpful things for the beginner that money cannot buy. First and foremost would be to find a seasoned veteran who will take you under his or her wing and keep you from purchasing unnecessary equipment or forming bad habits. Second, no book, regardless of how thorough, can duplicate the hands-on experience of trying out a variety of rods and learning how to cast with help from a professional instructor. Learning to cast properly is absolutely essential to angling enjoyment and success. University of Wisconsin biology professor and internationally recognized fly fishing lecturer and author, Gary Borger, feels that "the biggest mistake that beginners make is not spending enough time learning to cast properly." If you can't get the fly out on the water comfortably and precisely, fly fishing will be extremely frustrating, and you'll find it difficult, if not impossible, to catch fish.

If you have a sizeable financial investment in gear, it may be worth it to get your fishing tackle insured. The premium is minimal, and if theft or breakage occurs, at least you won't have to reach into your own pocket to cover the replacement cost.

Please remember that the lists in this chapter are general guidelines. As you gain experience, you will personalize your inventory of tackle and gear to include the essentials and extras that will refine the sport and truly make fly fishing pleasurable for you.

Spruce Creek

The true joy of pursuing trout is that they live in such beautiful places.

– Howell Raines

My fellow instructor Earl Shapiro summed up my feelings perfectly when he told Rich Roseborough the fly shop owner and me that he couldn't sleep the night before our first fly fishing school years ago. I had been excited and sleepless, too, just like a kid on Christmas Eve. Sunrise found me sleepy-eyed, but rarin' to go. I remember Rich and I went to the grocery store that morning, and it proved to be an interesting and memorable experience. Neither of us had food shopped for two dozen people before, but somehow we got through the maze of food aisles, and all the good-looking things to eat along the way. When finished, we painstakingly loaded the old Ford pickup, stopped to pick up Earl and headed off for what has become our "Fantastic Journey" four times each summer.

We selected Spruce Creek at Evergreen Farms as the locale for our school because it's one of America's premier trout streams. Wildlife, like the eastern wild turkey, ruffed grouse, black bear and white-tailed deer can be seen in the upper meadows or woods. Songbirds and familiar backyard birds like the barn swallow, blue jay, northern cardinal, cedar waxwing, black- capped chickadee, eastern bluebird, yellow warbler, house finch, red and white breasted nuthatch, purple martin, eastern meadowlark, red-winged blackbird, American tree sparrow, and Carolina wren fill the air. Birds of prey like the American kestrel, red-tailed hawk, turkey vulture, and osprey can often be seen overhead, and mallards and wood ducks stop over on their northern migration. In addition, the lower cottage section has enough water and facilities to comfortably accommodate 20 people. Quality bed and breakfasts are close-at-hand, as are the airport and shopping in nearby State College.

Last but not least, the creek flows through the beautiful Tussey Mountain Valley and, best of all, there are no distractions. No annoying pagers or cellular phones. Forget the nasty boss, demanding customers, or unrealistic quotas, deadlines and responsibilities. Nothing except the enjoyment of the sport and the sounds of nature and the creek awaits.

As Rich's dark brown clunker, loaded down with provisions, strained its way up the Laurel Hill Summit, the three of us had plenty of time to talk. By that I mean we ripped into everyone we knew, and when we were done with them, we started in on one another. That truck cab was no place for the thin-skinned or faint of heart. The nonstop teasing was interrupted only by frequent stops for donuts, gas, lunch, corn on the cob, snacks, and the need to wipe the tears from our eyes. I have never laughed so hard. The three of us were having more fun than grown men should be allowed to have.

We poked our heads out the open windows of the truck and strained to see the condition of the water as we crossed the Frankstown Branch of the Juniata River. It looked great! Our expectations heightened when we crossed Canoe Creek and saw that it, too, had perfect water level and clarity. The prospects for a great weekend never looked better.

We turned right onto Route 45 and headed down the mountain. By the time we caught our first glimpse of Camp Espy Farm and the picturesque Little Juniata River flowing through the sun-drenched valley, we could hardly control ourselves!

Passing through the quaint town of Spruce Creek, we could see the mouth of Spruce Creek at its confluence with the Little Juniata. Our handwritten map, now difficult to read because of all the folding and unfolding, indicated that we had less than five miles to go. Our excitement grew as we passed the entrance to the Indian Caverns and Spruce Creek came into full view to the right of the road.

"There it is!" Earl shouted suddenly. We could see the green roof and large brick chimney of the cottage in the distance. A puff of white smoke seemed to herald our arrival. The cottage is located on the westernmost edge of Wayne Harpster's property, and soon we could see the sparkling white barns and silos bearing the unmistakable logo of Evergreen Farms. We made a right turn down the dirt lane and pulled into the lot.

We parked quickly and rushed to get out of the truck. No one spoke as we gazed upon the grandeur of this fly fishing mecca. Rich, Earl, and I stood there totally captivated, as though we had never seen a trout stream before. We walked toward the creek slowly, reverently, as if entering the sanctuary of a church. The wind whispering through the hemlocks seemed to echo the voices of the greats of the sport: Brooks, Fox, Harvey, Hewitt and Marinaro who fished here over the years. We felt as though we were standing on hallowed ground.

Within moments, we heard a screen door squeak open and slam shut. We turned to see a woman walking toward us. "Howdy," she said. "My name is Sarah. I work for Mr. Harpster and live just across the way." We introduced ourselves and exchanged pleasantries as she led us into the Cottage.

The great room was huge and imposing. The walls and ceiling were covered with sheets of burnt umber-colored paneling, stained darker by years of smokey poker games and resonating with fantastic tales of fish and fishing. The hardwood floor appeared well-traveled, and the massive stones of the walk-in hearth looked warm and inviting. I could almost hear the fireside chats of General Dwight Eisenhower and President Jimmy Carter, both frequent visitors to this magnificent place. The room was filled with leather rockers, three sofas, two dinner tables, a dozen chairs, a server, and two breakfronts. A bearskin rug, mounted deer head, vintage clocks, and a 1982 Harpster Chevrolet calendar hung on the walls. The place even had an old black rotary phone. The four bedrooms, as well as the bath and kitchen, all extended from the great room. But, the most striking feature of the cottage couldn't be seen; it was felt. Call it aura, ambience, or what have you, the place just had a comfortable feel to it.

We soon heard the sound of gravel crunching under tires. Sarah told us that it must be Wayne, so Rich, Earl, and I went out to meet him. The valves rapped in the old Chevy Suburban as the driver shut off the engine, opened the door and spit an amber stream of Union Workman chewing tobacco. We introduced ourselves, and as we shook hands I could tell by his appearance and the conversation that Wayne Harpster was what you might affectionately call a "character."

He stood about 5 feet 10 inches tall, and had a stocky, muscular build. He wore traditional work clothes and a Harpster Chevrolet baseball cap that concealed a crew cut. His complexion and demeanor were as rugged as the work on the farm. He told us that he owned approximately 2,000 acres and leased an equal amount. With 2,000 head of milking Holsteins and 1,600 replacement Heifers, Evergreen Farms is one of Pennsylvania's largest dairy operations. Wayne said, "Three tankers a day leave the farm, and deliver approximately 138,000 pounds of unprocessed milk to dairy plants in North Carolina, Tennessee, and a couple other southern states." As much as Wayne seemed to enjoy talking about the business, though, his eyes sparkled when he told us about his stream. He explained that the prestigious Spruce Creek Rod and Gun Club separates the upper and lower sections of his property. Established in 1907, this private club has its own lodge with a full time housekeeper, stream keeper, trout hatchery, and four miles of blue ribbon water.

The upper section of Harpster's Spruce Creek meanders through an open meadow. It has many pools, excellent insect hatches, and holds a lot of fish. The rustic stone cabin is situated along the stream and was built in 1937. Renovated in 1990, it sleeps 12, has an equipped kitchen and a huge enclosed porch that overlooks the beautiful valley and stream.

Spruce Creek eventually flows past the Harpster homestead, built in 1813, through the club property, and then into the lower section where we conduct our school.

This lower section of the creek flows through pastures, fields, and along hillsides of ash, black locust, elm, dogwood, shagbark hickory, sugar maple, walnut and willow trees, and stands of hemlock along the bank at the base of Tussey Mountain. Dame's rocket, joe-pye weed, multiflora rose, spotted touch-me-not, Virginia creeper and other wildflowers grow in the fields and near the creek. This lower mile and a half of water consists of a dozen or so long, wadeable pools separated by dams. Much of the stream improvement was completed by Wayne 35 years ago. Every section is unique and challenging and is loaded with trout, including a healthy population of wild browns. The lower Cottage section has an abundance of predictable insect hatches too.

Midges, which are members of the order Diptera, can be seen on almost any sunny day during the year, but it's the little bluewinged olive dun, *Baetis tricaudatus,* which appears in March and April, that announces the coming of the new season. Crane flies, which are also in the order Diptera, hatch in the spring, as do grannom caddisflies, *Brachycentrus* spp., followed by the brown or tan winged caddisflies, in the family Hydropsychidae. The Sulphur, *Ephermerella rotunda,* provides exciting evening fishing starting in mid-May and continuing into early July. Blue quills, *Paraleptophlebia* spp., dance up and down near the banks all day long. They start appearing in mid-May too, and end in early fall. The chocolate dun, *Serratella deficiens,* can be seen in late May and will last into June. The green drake, *Ephemera guttulata,* is usually on the water by late May, and lasts up to ten days. Bluewinged olives, *Drunella cornuta,* the slate drakes, *Isonychia bicolor,* and light cahills, *Stenacron interpunctatum,* appear sporadically from early June and into July. In some sections of the creek, the yellow drake, *Ephemera varia,* can be seen. Micro caddisflies, in the family Hydroptilidae, as well as the little yellow stoneflies, *Isoperla* spp., hatch from early May through August. The summer-long terrestrial fishing, with imitations of members of the insect orders, Coleoptera (beetles), Hymenoptera (ants), and Orthoptera (grasshoppers and crickets) can't be beat. But it's the tiniest of the mayflies, the trico, *Tricorythodes* spp., for which Spruce Creek is famous. This diminutive insect brings up some of the largest fish in the creek to feed on the surface. The morning hatches and spinner falls start in mid-July and continue until the first hard frost sometime in mid-October. Last, fall fishing with the second broods of little bluewinged olive duns, *B.* tricaudatus, the slate drake, *I.* bicolor ends the year as it began.

In addition to the flora, fauna and superb year-round trout fishing, another interesting feature of this section is the authentic, mortise-and-tenon constructed covered bridge that is located near the Cottage. Built by Wayne, who used wood cut from trees on his farm, the bridge was finished by local Amish carpenters and was dedicated by President and Mrs. Jimmy Carter. The inscription on the brass plaque reads, "Designed and engineered by R. Wayne Harpster of Spruce Creek, the foundation of this covered bridge was constructed in 1979. Ten years later, using the historical 'post and beam' style, this covered bridge was constructed by Clarence 'Breezy' Dean with the help of men employed by Evergreen Farms. Joined by mortise, tenons and driven pegs, this bridge consists of oak, hemlock and white pine cut from the Harpster property and prepared at the family sawmill. The completion of this bridge on May 26, 1989 was assisted by President Jimmy Carter and his wife Rosalynn. A covered bridge celebration was given for family and friends, including President and Mrs. Carter. Following a christening by his mother Juliet E. Harpster, Wayne dedicated this bridge to his mother and in memory of his father, Robert L. Harpster."

After bidding Wayne goodbye, the three of us went back into the cottage. There on one of the coffee tables sat the guest registry. I picked it up and read through page after page of names and comments. I was struck by the number of visitors and the positive things they had to say. It appeared that no one had left disappointed, and we hoped all of our students would feel the same way.

Chapter Three

Fly Lines, Terminal Tackle And Knots

Not practicing efficient and quick knot tying for tippets and fly attachments is one of the biggest mistakes an angler can make.

– Dave Whitlock

You can own the finest tackle that money can buy and have all the time in the world to use it, but if you don't learn how to tie at least two of the three basic knots discussed in this chapter, you'll find it difficult, if not impossible, to fly fish.

But before you learn to tie anything, you need to know the components that make up the entire line: the backing, fly line, leader and tippet (Figure 3.1).

Backing

Backing is usually made from strands of Dacron braided together to increase strength while maintaining a thin, uniform diameter. It comes in traditional white or the new fluorescent colors. Backing serves three purposes. First, its thin diameter increases the line capacity of the reel, a feature that acts like insurance against a big fish taking all of the fly line and leaving you with nothing in reserve. Second, because the backing fills up the narrow inner portion of the reel spool, the fly line won't come off so tightly coiled, and third, increases the line pick-up speed.

Fly Lines

Although you can still purchase a traditional silk line, the vast majority of fly lines sold today, especially to beginners, are made from a strong core of braided nylon coated with polyvinyl chloride. All lines meet the American Fishing Tackle Manufacturers Association standards for thickness and taper and are approximately 30 yards long.

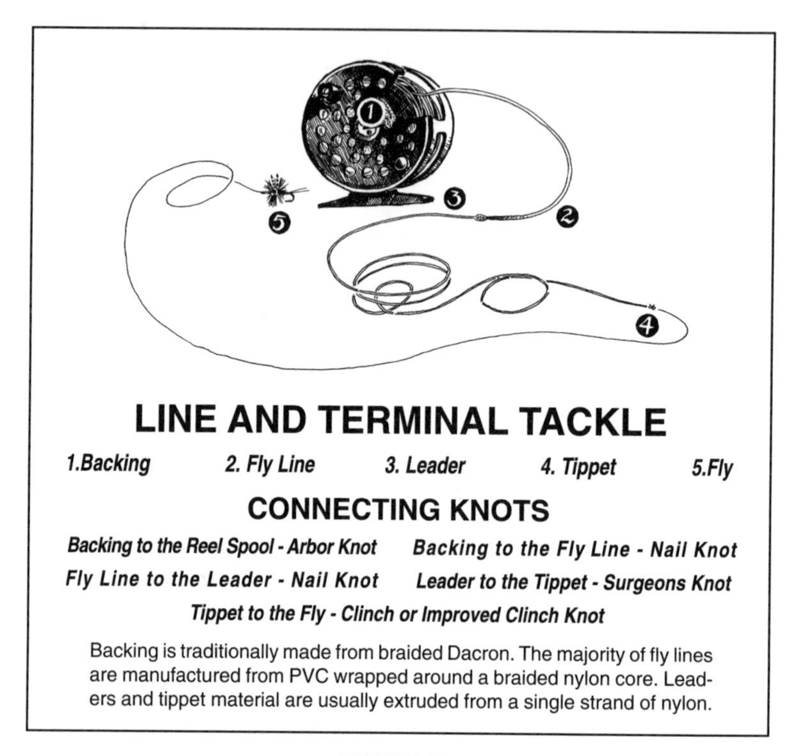

FIGURE 3.1

Taper means that the fly line varies in width to enhance casting. If you look at any fly line box, you will notice two capital letters followed by a one or two number designation printed boldly on the label. For example, you may see a WF6 or a DT10. The letters indicate the line taper: L = Level Line, DT = Double Taper, WF = Weight Forward (Figure 3.2). The number that follows specifies the weight in grains of the first 30 feet of the line. They range from 1-12 weight, and the smaller the number, the lighter and thinner the line and vice versa. Lighter lines (3 and 4 weight) are designed for narrow streams, small flies and delicate presentations. Midweight lines (5-7 weight) work best in bigger water where you need to use large flies or plan to fish under the surface. Heavy duty lines, size 8 and higher, are rarely used in trout fishing, and are primarily designed for bass, saltwater, salmon and steelhead angling.

Modern fly lines are made to float or sink and come in a variety of tapers. The weight forward (WF) and double taper (DT) are good choices for anyone just starting out. As a matter of fact, upwards of 95 percent of most shops' fly line sales are in these two categories.

The weight forward line is intended for those anglers who plan to use large flies and bass bugs. In addition, if you need to cast longer distances or into the wind, the WF line will serve you best. The double

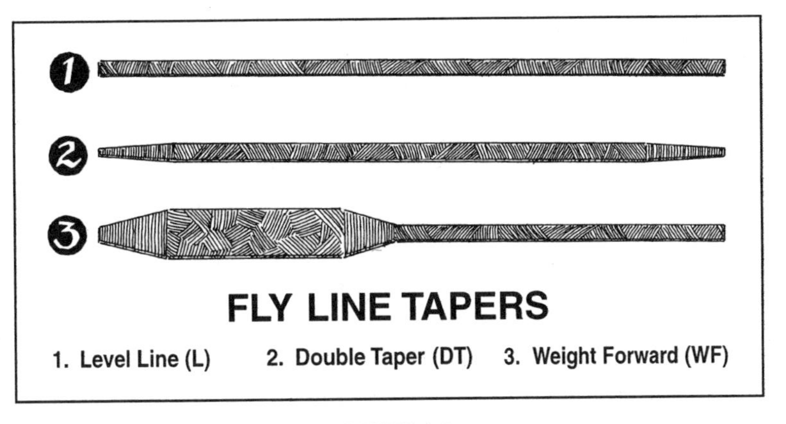

FIGURE 3.2

taper, in my opinion, is perfect for beginners because at normal distances of 30 to 40 feet it casts as easily as the WF and offers the economic benefit of being reversible when the front taper wears out.

The adhesive-backed line weight label that manufacturers supply with their fly lines should either be placed inside the reel on the back side of the spool, or placed on the underside of the reel foot. An alternative would be to systematically mark your fly line with a black waterproof felt-tipped pen. For example, you can make four short lines to identify the fly line as a 4 weight. It is important to do this because as time passes the factory sticker may become soiled or fall off. At some point, you will undoubtedly want to change fly lines, yet save or give away the old one. You won't have to trust your memory if the line is already marked. Finally, it is a good idea, especially if you're just starting out, to mark all of your fly lines at 30 and 40 feet, or at least identify the end of the front taper. This can be done with a Sharpie® pen or a laundry marker of contrasting color. These measurements are important to a beginner because they will provide an accurate gauge of casting length and better distance perception. It will also serve as a reminder that when the heaviest portion of the weight forward line is just beyond the rod tip, you can make the longest casts.

LEADERS

Leaders bridge the gap between the heavier, thicker fly line and the fly. They are traditionally made from clear nylon which is also referred to as monofilament. Braided nylon leaders are available, too, but in my opinion are not practical for beginners because they are difficult to maintain and expensive. Leaders come packaged singly and are sold knotless or knotted. Leaders are tapered by one of two processes. First, some are hand tied by using multiple transitional sections of decreasingly thinner monofilament.

Knotless styles, in contrast, are extruded from one piece of nylon and tapered by the manufacturer. Leaders are typically available in three basic lengths: 7, 9 and 12 feet. Care should be taken when removing one from the package so that the leader doesn't become tangled when you take it apart. After you open the package, slip the coiled leader around the fingers and thumb of one hand, then carefully unwind and unwrap the thicker butt end first until the entire leader comes apart easily.

Leaders have two numbers printed boldly on the package label. The first number indicates the length, and the second number, followed by an X, specifies the diameter at the end of the leader, the tippet. For example, a 7 feet 4X leader is 7 feet long and tapered to a 4X tippet. The higher the X designation, the thinner the tippet. A thinner tippet is used with lighter fly lines and smaller flies. Conversely, the lower the X designation, the thicker the tippet material. Thicker material is especially beneficial in subsurface fishing where bigger flies and lead shot to sink them is required, or in windy conditions.

Leader tapers follow time-tested formulas. They are thicker at the butt end where they are attached to the fly line, and taper out to the tippet where the fly is tied. Nationally recognized author, fly tier, master rod builder, and instructor Fran Betters contends that "one mistake that beginners often make is using too long a leader. This only leads to problems with turn over and wind knots."

A leader's length and taper directly affect the cast. There are literally dozens of different taper formulas, but they tend to fall into two general categories that are important to the beginning trout fishermen. First, a short leader of 7 feet and tapered to 3X or 4X is easier to cast and turns over better into the wind. This length and taper is ideal for use in subsurface fishing with wet flies, nymphs and streamers and lead shot, or when using larger wind resistant dry flies on top of the water. Longer leaders, 9 and 12 feet, tapered to 5X and 6X, are well suited for use in calm weather or in dry fly fishing where the trout are close to the surface and the fly and leader need to be presented delicately.

TIPPET

Nationally recognized fly fishing instructor, author and Vice President of Orvis®, Tom Rosenbauer, feels that "veterans and novice anglers alike don't pay enough attention to their tippet length and its diameter." The tippet is the thinnest section of the leader and is located at the end to which the fly is tied. It, too, is usually made from nylon, but differs from the rest of a knotless leader because it has no taper. Tippet material of various sizes is also used to construct hand-tied leaders. For that reason it is sold in spools of one uniform diameter. Tippet material comes in 30 yard spools in nine popular sizes, 0X (.011 inch diameter) to 8X (.0035 inch diameter), and is commercially available from a variety of manufacturers. Although each company's materials differ in color, strength, softness/stiffness, and abrasion resistance, by and large they are uniform in length and diameter and perform the same job. The spools have a numerical designation followed by an X. The number corresponds to diameter, and the X no longer has meaning.

If you are uncertain about the numeric size of your tippet, the "Rule of 11" is an easily remembered formula to help determine its diameter in thousandths of an inch. Simply subtract your tippet's X designation from eleven, and you'll know the exact numerical diameter. For example, a 5X tippet subtracted from 11 equals six or six thousandths (.006).

As a matter of environmental responsibility and common sense, please dispose of any unneeded quantities of tippet material or used leaders in a proper receptacle. On stream you can either cut up or roll up used material and throw it away later. Nylon is not biodegradable; consequently, fish, birds or small animals could become entangled in it, suffer needlessly or even die.

KNOTS

There are three basic knots that every beginner needs to master: the clinch knot, the surgeon's knot and the nail knot, with the first two being the most important. Traditionally, these are some of the easiest knots to learn to tie. There are other equally good knots that can be substituted, and if you are already comfortable tying a different one, there is no need to change.

The clinch knot is used to attach the fly to the end of the tippet. But before you learn to tie it, I would like to tell you about a useful gadget that pays for itself over and over again.

The E-Z Mini Hook® Tool (Figure 3.3) will prove to be one of the most indispensable accessories in your vest. You can use it to grasp and pull out any size fly from your box, and it is especially useful in holding the smaller ones. If you accidentally drop the tool, you can easily see it and pick it up, saving you the expense and aggravation of losing a fly. In addition, it can also be used to hold the fly while making the turns necessary to tie the clinch knot. Another benefit to using the tool is that you don't get stuck by the hook point as often. Modify your E-Z Mini Hook® Tool by adding a cork sleeve, and it will even float!

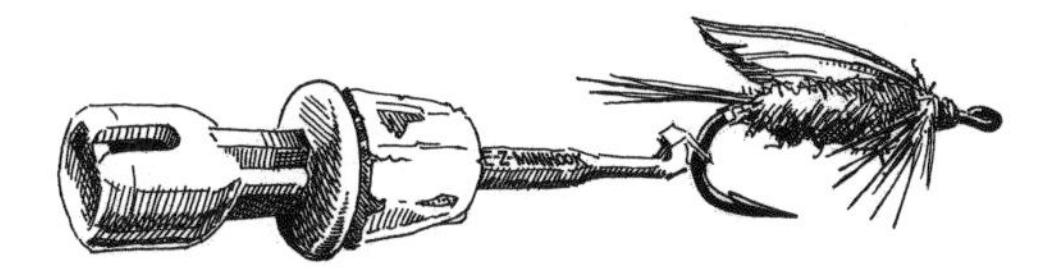

FIGURE 3.3

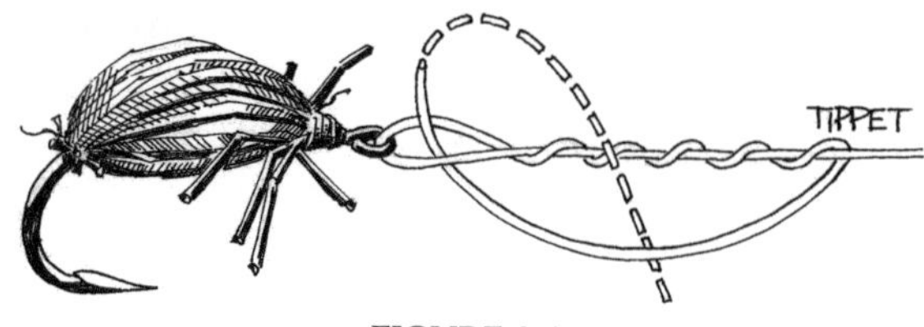

FIGURE 3.4

The Clinch Knot

The clinch knot is one of the strongest and most reliable knots used to attach a fly to the tippet.

The instructions for tying the clinch knot (Figure 3.4) are as follows:

1. Remove the fly from the fly box and place it at its bend in the E-Z Mini Hook® Tool with the body of the hook parallel to the shaft of the tool.

2. Insert the end of the tippet through the eye of the hook, otherwise known as the tag, and extend it five to six inches. It makes no difference whether you thread the tippet up or down through the eye. Cutting the end of the tippet at an angle will make it easier to thread through the hook eye. This is especially true in the smaller hook sizes.

3. Double over this end, now referred to as the tag, and hold it directly underneath and parallel to the long end of the tippet between the index finger and thumb near the eye of the hook. This will form the important loop necessary to tie this knot.

4. Grasp the tag end in your opposite hand, between the index finger and thumb, and turn it clockwise away from your hands and around the tippet. To complete the circle, grasp the tag end as it comes around with the middle and fourth finger of the hand holding the fly, or twist the E-Z Mini Hook® Tool while pinching the tippet and tag.

5. Continue turning until you've completed five wraps, counting each wrap as you turn. Then, lift the thumb of the hand holding the fly and pass the tag end, from behind, up and through the loop referred to in step three.

6. Lubricate the knot with saliva, hold on to the tag end and tighten it by gently pulling the long end of the tippet until it is snug.

7. When the knot is nearly tight, release the tag end, cinch the knot tight by pulling the long end, then pull the tag end and finish the knot by cutting the tag end flush. A well-tied knot will not slip; therefore, there is no need for an extended tag end.

8. Test the knot against the spring of the E-Z Mini Hook® Tool. If the knot comes apart, cut off the tag end and start over.

To tie the improved knot, follow this next step after you finish step five. We will designate this step 5A.

5A. A second loop is formed after you perform step five. Through this second loop pass the tag end up and back through, away from your hands, hold, lubricate, and tighten the knot by following steps 6, 7 and 8.

It is important to match the tippet diameter to the fly you intend to use. If you choose a fly that is too large, three problems can occur: first, the oversized fly can twist and weaken the delicate tippet; second, the leader will not turn over and present the fly properly, and third, a fly that is too big can snap off when cast.

Beginners often find it difficult to differentiate between fly sizes. Size designations always refer to hook length. The most popular fly sold today is a size 14 which is approximately 1/2 inch long. If you are unsure about the size of a fly, simply take a piece of 1/2 inch wide Scotch® tape, and circle it around your rod shaft just ahead of the grip. You now have a guide by which to measure a size 14 hook! A size 14 almost splits the ordinary freshwater fly hook selection in half. By adding or subtracting 1/8 inch, you can approximate the length of the remaining standard sizes from 2 through 28.

Fly fishermen in general often question what size tippet to use. The "Rule of 3" is a generalized formula to help determine an approximate tippet diameter for a given hook size. Simple divide the fly size by three. For example, a size 18 fly divided by three, equals six, or a 6x tippet.

Changing flies can be challenging for a beginner, especially if you don't know the diameter of the existing tippet or the size of the next fly. This situation can be made even more frustrating if you forget how to tie the knot. Therefore, it is important to learn and memorize all the information and formulas that we discuss in this chapter. You can carry a knot tying book in your fishing vest if you are the least bit uncertain.

The Surgeon's Knot

During the course of a day on stream you will probably lose a fly or two, and if you are anything like me, you'll lose a lot more. In addition, you may

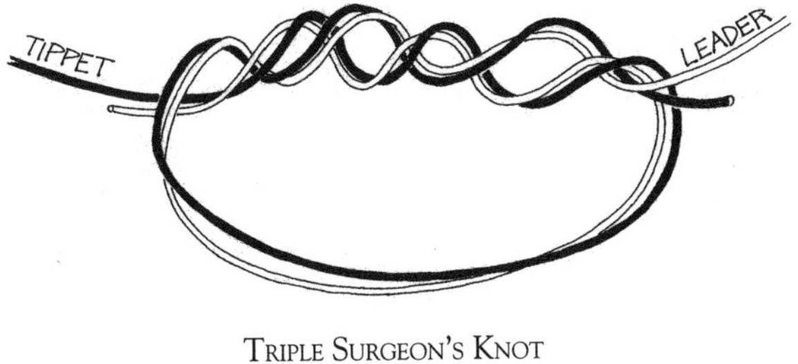

Triple Surgeon's Knot
FIGURE 3.5

want to change patterns or try a different size. Changing flies will shorten the tippet to the point that you will eventually need to replace it.

A good knot to use for adding tippet to the existing leader, or making a hand-tied leader, is the surgeon's knot (Figure 3.5), and it can be tied in two variations: the double or the triple. Regardless of which you choose, a leader gauge (micrometer) will indicate the optimum place to add on tippet and tie the new knot. A leader gauge/micrometer is an accessory that measures the diameter of monofilament, and it is available at fly tackle dealers or a precision tool shop.

The instructions for tying the surgeon's knot are as follows:

1. Cut off the old tippet and gauge the size of the existing leader. To determine the leader's diameter, measure approximately 3 inches from the tag end.

2. Remove a $2^1/_2$ -foot piece of tippet material that is no thicker than three thousandths of an inch.

3. Overlap 5 inches of either end of the tippet onto the last 3 inches of the leader. You now have two tag ends and two long ends extending in opposite directions. Hold them together firmly between the thumb and index finger of the hand closest to the tag end (short end) of the tippet. Now you have the two ends necessary to tie this knot: the short end of the leader and the long end of the tippet, overlapping each other by 4 inches or so.

4. Grasp the material closest to the tag end of the tippet in your hand. Turn both pieces simultaneously toward the hand holding the material and to the front forming a small loop. Tuck and hold the loop firmly between the thumb and fingers of the hand referred to in step three, the one holding the loop.

5. From behind the loop, first bring the short tag end of the leader up and through; then bring the long end of the tippet up and through and hold them firmly together. If you've done it correctly, you have formed an upside down overhand knot, just like the first knot you make when tying your shoes.

6. To tie the double surgeon's knot, simply repeat step five. To tie the triple, repeat step five a third time.

7. Lubricate and tighten the knot initially by pulling all four pieces simultaneously. To cinch it down, let go of the two short tag ends, relubricate if necessary and pull the two long ends steadily in opposite directions. To finish the knot, repeat that same procedure with the two short tag ends. Lubrication is essential because friction can burn the material. If tied properly, the tag ends will extend away from one another. If they hang down side by side or the knot slips or pulls apart, the knot has been tied incorrectly. Start over and pay closer attention to step four which is where a mistake is often made.

During the excitement and anticipation of fishing, it's easy to cut the wrong piece of material. You can ensure that this won't happen by getting into the habit of holding the two long ends in your hand. This allows the two tag ends to stick up so that they can be easily identified and trimmed.

Please note that when adding tippet to your existing leader you do not want to decrease the size more than three thousandths of an inch. If you must, add a transition section(s) or a new tippet as you would when changing from a large fly to a smaller one. Always continue the taper following that same rule.

When you purchase a new reel, line, and leader, most fly shops will rig them at no charge. As a result, most people never see the arbor knot[3] that holds the backing to the reel spool, nor do they see the knot that joins both the backing and the leader to the fly line. The latter two are identical and are called nail knots.

The Nail Knot

Old-timers used a nail to tie this knot, hence the name. As the years passed, fishermen substituted a needle, which pulls the material through, or a tube that allows you to pass it manually (Figure 3.6).

FIGURE 3.6

The instructions for tying the nail knot are as follows:

1. Hold the end of the fly line horizontal in either direction and double over a 6 to 8 inch piece of backing or leader. This will give you three individual pieces of material. The first piece is the end of the fly line, or tag end. The second is the short end, also designated as a tag end of the doubled over leader or backing, and the third is the long end of either the leader or backing. Add a small tube[4] to those three and hold

3. The arbor knot is used to attach backing to the reel spool. The directions to tie it are as follows: Tie and overhand knot in the end of the backing, trim that end flush and pass it around the arbor of the spool. Using that tag end, tie another overhand knot around the long end of the backing. Draw the second overhand knot tight, and allow it to slip down against the first overhand knot and the arbor.

4. Use a hollow plastic Q-tip® with the ends cut off approximately one and one half inch in length. The plastic material is sturdy and inexpensive.

all four pieces firmly in one hand.

2. Take the short tag end of the backing or the leader and wind it clockwise, away from the hand holding the tube, and around all four pieces. When you have made five or six turns, tuck that tag end into the tube and push it back toward the palm of your hand. Once the material is completely through the tube continue to push the tube backward and out and put it aside.

3. Keeping firm pressure on the wraps between your thumb, index, and middle fingers, alternately pull the tag end of the backing or leader and then the long end until you feel the knot start to tighten.

4. At this point gently let go of the knot and realign any overlapped wraps normally found in the leader. Grasp the tag end and the long end of the backing or leader, lubricate, and pull steadily in opposite directions until the knot is cinched down.

5. Grasp the long end of the backing or leader and the long end of the fly line and pull steadily in opposite directions to finish tightening the knot.

6. Finally, cut the tag ends as close to the knot as possible and use a drop of Krazy Glue® to permanently bond them together. Tying the nail knot can be simplified by using the Tie-Fast Knot Tyer® manufactured by Sierra Stream and Mountain. This handy tool comes with instructions that make it easy to use.

Beginners can also try a loop-to-loop leader connection instead of the nail knot. Once you learn to tie a surgeon's loop[5] and connect the loops on the leader and fly line correctly, changing leaders, especially on stream, can be made dramatically easier. However, it has been my experience that a loop-to-loop leader connection tends to be less aerodynamic, and the fly can easily snag on it.

Knots are the weakest links between fish and fisherman. The ones I have discussed here will serve you well in all types of trout fishing. However, as you gain experience and begin to fish for larger quarry, you need to reconsider the knots you are using. For example, the Albright knot, which can be used to join the backing to the fly line, never fails. Conversely, when fighting heavier fish a nail knot can slip and fail by actually pulling the PVC coating off the nylon core.

Making your own leaders is good training for a beginner because it forces you to think, follow directions, and learn to tie knots. Practicing indoors during the winter under pleasant conditions is ideal.

Last, I would like to discuss some practical information regarding knots and leaders.

5. The surgeon's loop is tied by doubling over the last six inches of the thick butt end of the leader. Make two consecutive overhand knots in the doubled material, lubricate, tighten and cut the tag end flush.

• If you think that you have tied a knot improperly, assume that you have and start over. Take your time to do it right the first time. Re-tying knots is time consuming, frustrating, and increases the chances of your doing it wrong again. This is one of the best pieces of advice I can give you.

• It is important to tie with generous amounts of material because long tag ends are easier to handle and cinch down when tying onstream, especially if it's cold, windy or dark. A knot isn't finished until the tag ends are tightened.

• Count aloud if necessary to ensure the prescribed number of wraps. This is especially true for knots that require an equal or specific number of turns. Lefty Kreh agrees and explains that "if five turns are recommended with the tag end around the main line, use five turns. If you use six turns, you may have too many turns to enable you to draw the knot tight. If you use four turns, then there may not be enough turns to hold the connections securely."[6]

• Unless you store your tippet material properly, you should use new tippet material each season, especially the thinner diameters. The strength of monofilament can be adversely affected by light, heat, and cold. Remember that monofilament is one of the least expensive investments that you will make in this sport. According to Lefty, "Tippet material should be stored in a cool place, not excessively dry, and never exposed to light, especially fluorescent light, for long periods of time."

• It is a good idea to use tippet material made by the same company that produced your leaders because the manufacturing process for both is consistent in the important characteristics of stiffness, strength and diameter. Lefty further contends that using materials of similar limpness is important. He points out that "some people unwisely use hard or a stiff monofilament in the butt section of a leader, then try to connect it to a much limper strand. Anyone who has attempted that knows that it's somewhat like tying a rubber band to limp wire."[7]

• Tighten and test all knots slowly and evenly and lubricate them with saliva, or you can wet your fingers in the stream and then moisten the knot. If after you test it your knot slips or pulls apart, cut the tag end(s) off and start over. Do not use your thumbnails or a hemostat to cinch down knots tied with monofilament. Either one could stress, scar or otherwise crimp the material. This common error can lead to many failures as can the injudicious use of a rubber line straightener which can weaken the leader through excessive heat caused by friction.

• A broken leader can tell you a lot about where and why the fail-

6. From the periodical, *Mid Atlantic Fly Fishing Guide*, July 1996 issue, page 20.

7. loc.cit.

ure occurred. For example, if the monofilament is cleanly severed, it suggests that the breakage is due to one of the following factors: a manufacturer's imperfection in the material; prior damage caused by a nick, bruise or a burn; or a break at the stress riser immediately adjacent to a knot. A curled end indicates slippage prior to the breaking of an improperly tied or tightened knot.

• Wind knots, which should be called casting knots, are caused by the tailing loop of a poorly executed cast. The resulting overhand knot, most often found in the tippet, can reduce the strength of the leader by as much as 50 percent. Rather than waste valuable onstream time by trying to pick it apart and further weakening the monofilament, simply cut off the old tippet and tie on a new one.

• Using a leader gauge will indicate a good point where the new tippet should be added to the existing leader. This spot is located at a position where the new tippet diameter will not decrease the end of the leader more than three thousandths of an inch. When tippet material needs to be added, do so at the correct position with a lubricated knot. Tighten the knot slowly and evenly and then trim the tag ends flush.

According to research done by Lefty Kreh and fishing expert Mark Sosin, knots slip before they break. Following that line of thinking, leaders that have fewer knots and knots with fewer wraps, should have less potential for slippage. Therefore, the opportunity for breakage must decrease, too. Though the differences may be small, knotless leaders are more aerodynamic, less likely to be affected by varying currents, and don't pick up as much debris when fished, especially under the surface.

• It is important to check your line and leader connections as well as the length and condition of the tippet before you leave home. Doing so will save you valuable time better spent fishing than repairing a leader on stream.

• Knots can lose up to 10 percent of their strength in the 24-hour period[8] after they have been tied. Therefore, knots should be re-tightened before each use. This practice will also help to straighten the leader.

• Unless you are certain how to construct a leader properly, I discourage the use of hand-tied leaders with multiple transitional sections. Beginning fly fishermen should use factory manufactured knotless leaders. However, as you gain experience, learning to tie your own leaders will enhance your knot tying ability as well as your understanding of leader dynamics.

---

8. From the book, *Practical Fishing Knots* by Kreh & Sosin. The 1972 edition, page 16.

If you absolutely insist on making your own leaders[9], I suggest the 60-20-20 leader proportion formula. Sixty percent of the leader should be in the butt section(s), 20 percent in the transitional section(s), and 20 percent in the tippet. Remember that you should not decrease the size more than three thousandths of an inch (.003) when adding transitional sections or tippet onto the existing leader. Anglers are setting up disproportionate stress when they add a smaller diameter tippet to the larger diameter existing leader because the ends being joined are of unequal strength. Since the knot is stronger than the material with which it is tied and is often joined at the wrong place, it is little wonder that monofilament lines break.

After 15 years of teaching fly fishing, I have found that far too often fly fishermen reach a certain level of proficiency and then simply quit learning. They attend a school, catch some fish, and believe they know it all. Or they don't go to school and still think they know it all. You know that old-timer who's been doing it the same way for years? Is it possible that he or she has been doing it wrong all that time? Using knots which are dependable and simple to tie can only be an asset. Why not utilize every advantage, no matter how small, to make your fishing experience as pleasant and successful as possible.

Remember, the most important objective for any fly fisherman, but especially a beginner, is to use reliable knots that can be tied consistently under any conditions.

9. *Trout Volume 1,* written by Ernest Schwiebert and *Fishing Dry Flies for Trout: on Rivers & Streams,* written by Art Lee are two excellent resources for leader taper information.

Some Memorable Students

Fishermen are almost as interesting as the fish themselves!

– John Gierach

To the best of my recollection, I have helped teach hundreds of students over the past 15 years at the Roseborough School[10] on Spruce Creek. A few of them were humdingers.

There was the "Soldier of Fortune," for example, who showed up on the first Saturday morning dressed in full jungle camouflage battle fatigues. I suspect he must have served and been wounded in Vietnam because he had a noticeable limp and wore braces on the outside of his clothing. There seemed to be something troubling his mind, too. Later that morning, I was giving some casting instruction in the upper meadow when I saw him coming toward me. I politely said "hello," but hoped he would just keep walking because I found him to be most unsettling. However, he stopped and struck up a conversation. The two of us sat on a huge stone next to the Willow Pool. We reminisced about the '60s and our military experiences. When I mentioned that I was thirsty, he immediately jumped to his feet, removed his fishing vest, and pulled out a cold six-pack of *my* beer that he obviously had taken from the refrigerator in the cottage. I accepted his offering and thanked him as he went on his way. Well, at least I salvaged one can of my beer!

A fellow showed up one Saturday looking as sober as an oldtime preacher delivering a fire and brimstone sermon. It appeared as though he had all his worldly possessions hermetically sealed in Tupperware containers: food, clothing and most of his fishing gear, too. Apparently, all the members of his family must have gone to one of those parties and bought everything in stock.

At noon the dinner bell rang, and everyone came in except this man. He continued fishing the tail end of the President's Pool right next to the Instructor's Cottage. It was time for lunch, and all of the other

10. The Roseborough School is a comprehensive weekend course on fly fishing for trout. Classes are held on legendary Spruce Creek near State College in Central Pennsylvania. Information can be obtained by writing to South Hills Rod & Reel, 3227 W. Liberty Ave., Pittsburgh, PA 15216; or by phoning (412) 344-8888.

students were standing around watching him fish. It didn't appear as though he was coming in to eat any time soon. Earl had a clever idea; he got a donut, while Rich wrote a short message inviting the man to come in for lunch. I put the donut and the message into one of his Tupperware bowls, carefully sealed the lid and threw the bowl into the water. As luck would have it, the current carried the bowl right down to him. He picked it up, opened the lid and read the note. Laughing, he finally came in to eat.

A sparkling Cadillac pulled into the parking lot. Once the car had been parked, a tall, handsome young man got out of the driver's side. As he strolled toward me I sensed a refinement and elegance about him. He was impeccably dressed, appearing as if he had just stepped out of the Abercrombie & Fitch catalog. As we greeted each other and shook hands, I could tell by his demeanor and speech that he was educated and very well mannered. I walked back to his car to help him unpack. When he opened the trunk, I saw that he had the finest tackle money could buy. He showed me one beautiful Leonard bamboo rod after another and a collection of reels that was highlighted by an exquisite Edward VomHofe Perfectionist that must have cost thousands of dollars.

Later that morning, I was working with two students in the pool above the bridge when suddenly, from 100 yards away, I heard the most bloodcurdling screams coming from inside the cottage. I immediately dropped my rod and started running across the lawn. With each step I took, the shrieks became louder, and I was convinced that someone had suffered a heart attack. I seemingly flew through the door only to discover that same young gentleman at the point of tears, kneeling and searching for something on the floor. It was the most pathetic sight I had ever seen–a grown man lamenting the loss of a collarbutton-sized metal clicker that apparently had fallen off his priceless VomHofe reel. He kept on ranting and raving in spite of my efforts to console him. Nothing anyone said or did seemed to help. As time went on, he became more despondent and his determination more resolute. By now a dozen people were on all fours, inside and out, looking for the lost part. Without warning, the man sprang to his feet, ran out the door, went straight to his car, and with tires screeching he backed out of the lot and sped up the driveway. Totally puzzled, we all shrugged our shoulders, and I went back to my students.

An hour later I saw his speeding car off in the distance, heading in our direction. The Cadi turned down the driveway, into the parking lot and skidded to a dusty stop. The young man hurriedly got out of the car, opened the trunk and pulled out a military-style metal detector complete with earphones. Hundreds of holes later, it seemed as though he had dug up the entire front lawn in a futile attempt to find the missing part. Disgusted and depressed, he finally gave up. Without a word, he threw the metal detector into the car and drove away.

Two attorneys attended the first Roseborough School and provided us with engaging conversation and lively entertainment. On Saturday afternoon, the entire class was sitting on the porch finishing lunch and watching a handful of rising trout rhythmically feeding in the Home Pool in front of the Cottage. I could tell that everyone out there was eager to catch them, including the lawyer sitting across from me.

As I peered through the smoke that rose from his huge cigar, I could see the "skyscraper" of empty beer cans on the table in front of him and the determined look in his eye. He staggered to his feet, put on his straw hat and clamped the stogie between his clenched teeth. Grabbing his beer can and fly rod, he made his way stiff-legged to the edge of the water. He wobbled a little as he promptly put his first cast into the hemlocks on the opposite bank. Rather than unsnag the fly from shore, he decided to wade across the creek. Half way there, he instantly disappeared beneath the surface, his straw hat floating momentarily like a buoy marking the spot where he went down. Suddenly, he sprung up out of the water, slapped the hat back on his head, and went to work unsnagging the fly. When he finished, the "legal beagle" climbed out of the water, shook himself off and stormed over toward his van. Ten minutes later he reappeared wearing dry clothes and proclaiming to the assembly that he hadn't lost a drop of beer, his cigar stayed lit, and he found the fly plus a dozen other good ones, too!

My favorite dentist fancies himself quite the bamboo rod maker. His first attempt I christened, "The Old Sixty-Six." It was a six-foot, six-weight club that St. Patrick could have used to beat the snakes out of Ireland. In addition to its unusual combination of length and line weight, it featured a corkscrew tip section. Obviously, the individual sections had twisted when he glued and bound them together. Doc, who was fishing with us one weekend, came in frantic that Saturday afternoon with a tale that he told to all who would listen. He had hooked a five-pound brown and fought it for what seemed to be hours, he said. The fish took incredibly long runs and leaps, exhausting both fisherman and tackle. Rather than run the risk of breaking his new rod, Doc cut the fly line and let the monster get away! How's that for a fish story?

This character is my personal dentist, and at the risk of undergoing future procedures without the properly administered dose of novocaine, I must tell you that his subsequent cane creations have improved. However, my advice to him is, "Doc, you had better keep your day job!"

Sunday morning of that first weekend I was paired with a husband and wife who looked as though they were stepping onto the first tee at some posh country club. They were a delightful couple to teach, but they shared one vest and one rod and reel. Neither wore wading boots. They were newlyweds in love, and they were having a really good time. Off we went, the three of us, to the upper meadow. They were really casting quite well for beginners, so I left them alone to start back downstream to check on some of the other students. Suddenly I heard their shouts of joy. They had caught a fish! All four hands were on the rod at once as they dragged in the weary trout and threw it back into the creek. In the excitement of the moment they had obviously forgotten all about me. She leaped into his arms, locked her legs around his waist, and, I am embarrassed to say, the happy couple gave the congratulatory kiss a whole new meaning.

Later that afternoon I had an opportunity to slip away to do some fishing. All of the students were in another class, so off I went alone, or so I thought. My anticipation and excitement grew as I looked upstream and saw a handful of fish rising to the surface to feed. I discovered a huge brown trout sipping midges on the far bank above the bridge. I knelt down, tied on a Griffith's Gnat, made a few false casts and presented the fly. I could see the fish rising to take my offering when I felt someone tap me on the shoulder. I missed the fish's strike as I turned to see one of my students. Obviously he had decided to cut class and fish, too. There he stood with his fly line in one hand and a new leader in the other. "Could you help me?" he asked pathetically. Rather than replacing the tippet, this man was replacing the entire leader because he couldn't remember how to tie a surgeon's knot. He further confessed to forgetting how to tie the nail knot, too!

After all was said and done, we considered our inaugural school a success. To cap off the splendid weekend my fellow instructors and I decided to stop at Hughie's Lounge. The restaurant looked pretty run down from the outside, but it was getting late and we were hungry. I tried to look inside, but the windows were clouded by years of smoke and grease. There were dozens of cars outside, so we took a chance and went in.

What we didn't realize was that it was Sunday night and the Holy Ghost Tabernacle just up the street shared the same parking lot with the restaurant. Once inside the door, our worst fears were realized. There were only a handful of customers, and the place looked lost in the '50s. A slightly overweight, yet distinguished and well dressed man met us at the bar. He introduced himself as Hughie, and seemed quite pleased to see us. When he smiled, the whole room appeared to light up, due in part to the gleam of his gold crowns and the sparkle from the diamond rings that he sported on many of his fingers. He looked to be in his 60s, had a full head of silver hair and a thin well-trimmed mustache the same color. Hughie turned sideways to get through the narrow bar opening, escorted us into the dining room and told us that Babs would be over to take our order.

The walls hadn't seen a cleaning or a coat of paint in years. Dusty stuffed trout and black and white photo's of family reunions hung on the walls. Each table had a miniature Seeburg jukebox terminal hanging on the wall and was covered with a red and white check plastic tablecloth that was sticky to the touch. Notwithstanding, Rich, Duke and I decided to stay and piled into the corner booth. I knew we were in trouble when I thought I saw something crawl across the floor, but our waitress was the clincher.

Babs stood in front of us with one hand on her hip and the other adjusting her scarf. She tapped her foot to the beat of Bill Haley's hit song, "Rock Around the Clock," which was playing in the background. Her manicured fingernails were so shiny that I could almost read the menu in their reflection. She wore bobby socks and saddle oxfords and a short gingham cloth uniform that matched the tablecloth. A small white apron circled her aging waist and was tied in the back into a large bow. Her bleached blonde hair was pulled up into a beehive, and a small starched organdy cap was pinned on top. She wore at least a pound of makeup, horn-rimmed glasses, and false eyelashes that nearly touched her forehead. Cracking her chewing gum, she looked straight at me and through her puckered red lips spouted, "What il' it be chubby?" It was all downhill from there. The only thing worse than the food was the tip that I left her!

Two hours and a bottle of Tums® later, we were back home. As much as I loved our first school, the students, and all the fun we had, I found my own bed a welcome relief! As my head hit the pillow I gave thanks for the experience and said to myself, "I'll work on my wounded ego in the morning."

Chapter Four

The Casting Clinic

When you make a cast and can watch the fly line unroll symmetrically . . . it is a thing of beauty. The fly line is like a musical note, extended and held, in that it reaches out but remains attached to you. A beautiful cast has a practical side too, in that good loops of the right width can deliver a fly of any character to the target area in a way that makes the fly instantly fishable.

– Joan Salvato Wulff

It's a challenge to learn fly casting from a book, but I want to share some thoughts and insights with you that will better prepare you for this important and pleasurable portion of your fly fishing experience. In my opinion, casting a fly line is the most enjoyable aspect of this sport. In addition, improving your presentation techniques is immensely rewarding as you develop your skill and catch more fish.

Unlike spin casting in which a heavy bait is used to pull a weightless line, fly casting uses a heavy line to pull a weightless bait, or fly.

Fly casting can be described as the synchronous use of arm and rod to manipulate a line and propel an artificial fly where the angler desires. It is not difficult, but it is important to get professional instruction, practice what you learn, and be patient with yourself. Author, rod maker and respected fly fishing instructor Fran Betters reinforces this point when he says, "Fly casting is fun, and is not nearly as difficult as many have made it out to be."

I must advise you, however, not to judge all of fly fishing by your first experience. Many people learn to cast on a pond, in a field, a gymnasium or a parking lot. Unfortunately, none of these places can prepare you for the conditions you will find on a trout stream where the current is constantly moving. There will be a difference, so try not to become too frustrated when you finally get to the water.

When students in our weekend schools watch the casting video and observe the instructors, they come away with the impression that casting a fly line is simple to do. Not surprisingly, however, even our strongest and most athletic students have had their share of difficulty learning how to cast properly. Now, before the class goes to the casting pond, I teach them a new word, "physnesse." Physnesse is a neologism coined from the words physical and finesse. To cast a fly line efficiently takes a combination of both. Anyone can learn to do it, but casting is a physical exercise, and it takes a modicum of strength to snap the line off the water or ground, keep it in the air, and then present it to the water or ground again. It also requires timing, hand/eye coordination and finesse in regard to presentation. However, keep in mind that like every other sport, this one, too, has fundamentals that need to be understood and practiced. Remember, once you learn the basics, the techniques of casting a fly line will be the same regardless of the tackle you use or where you go to fish.

The Grip

Before you learn about the mechanics of fly casting, let's discuss how to hold the rod. I refer to the basic hand position as the "primary" or "thumb on top" grip (Figure 4.1). The thumb lies directly on top of the grip, aligned with the rod shaft, and on the side of the rod opposite the reel, while the fingers wrap comfortably and securely around the grip. I recommend this traditional hand position to everyone, but especially to beginners because it allows you to take advantage of the strongest muscles in the hand; the Phenar and Interossei. A variation of this grip is to substitute the index finger for the thumb. However, many fishermen find this alternative tiring. It is inherently weaker and almost impossible to use with heavy rods.

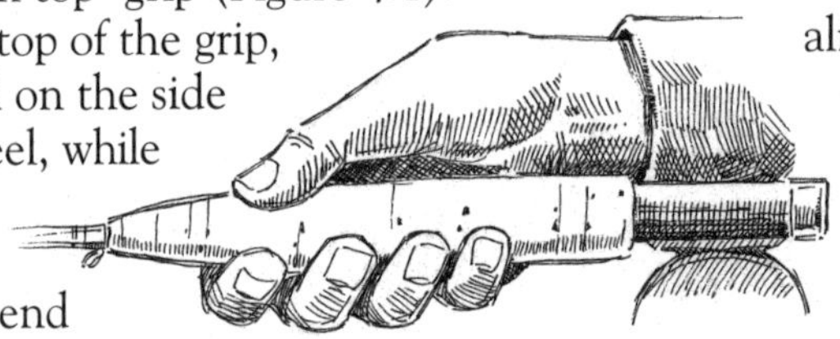

FIGURE 4.1

Another grip that some instructors teach is the "V grip." This hand position is similar to the way you would shake someone's hand, hold a screwdriver, or a tube of lipstick. This hand position is very comfortable, but for a beginner it will be more difficult to control unwanted wrist movement.

To recap, cradle the rod grip at the base of your fingers as if holding a suitcase handle and keep your flexed thumb on top of the grip. It's important to keep the reel directly under your wrist. Doing so will help keep your hand, wrist and forearm aligned, making it easier to perform the backward and forward snaps and stops of the fly rod.

Grip Pressure

How firmly should you hold the rod grip? You will prevent your hand, arm and shoulder from becoming prematurely fatigued by not squeezing the grip too tight. When I analyzed my own hand position, I discovered that only the thumb pad maintains constant pressure on the grip. The rest of the thumb remains arched in a flexed position on top of the rod grip. Begin by holding the rod as gently as though you were cradling a live bird as you initially lift the rod. Next, the muscles in your hand will voluntarily tighten on the grip as you snap and stop the rod.

THE WRIST

In 15 years of teaching fly fishing to beginners, I have seen every student make the same few common mistakes. First, most start casting with a straight arm, gently raising the rod tip causing slack line to drape in front of them. To catch up to the rod going up and back, they cock their wrists (radial deviation) throwing the fly line over and down, not up and back (Figure 4.2). The floppy wrist becomes the loose connection between the rod and forearm. Nationally acclaimed instructor and author Al Caucci finds that "beginners have a tendency to cast with their wrist only, instead of their forearm, resulting in a weak, open loop. Wrist casting leads to back cast rod position that ends at 9 o'clock, thus the loop is open and no power is generated in the forward cast."

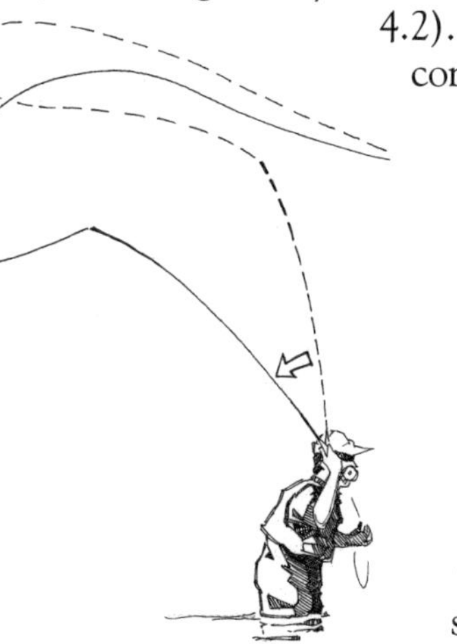

FIGURE 4.2

In my opinion, this casting error represents the biggest single mistake that every newcomer makes. If you want to learn to cast properly, it is imperative that you understand this point and develop the fundamental skills discussed throughout this chapter.

The second mistake most students make is that they try to cast too far by overpowering the final presentation cast. Professor George Harvey told me, "I have fished everywhere including the big rivers out West. Ninety-five percent of the trout that I caught were within thirty to thirty-five feet." In an effort to cast farther, beginners invariably apply too much power too soon in the forward presentation stroke which causes the rod tip to follow a concave path. This casting error "shocks" the fly rod and produces a tailing loop in which the leader drops below the level of the fly line often creating wind knots. Wind knots, which we discussed in chapter three, dramatically weaken the leader. Please remember that the final forward presentation stroke needs to be as smooth as the backward and forward casts that preceded it and made with the same amount of power.

Think about throwing a dart, swatting a fly, or driving a nail. Focus on these mental pictures in regard to moving your wrist and arm. Remember, all of these actions have a few things in common. To be done effectively, they must be executed smoothly, with control and with the release in a straight line at just the right moment.

LOAD AND LOOPS

Author, instructor and Pennsylvania State University fly fishing Professor Emeritus Joe Humphreys believes that "one of the bigger problems that beginners face is the inability to control casts for accuracy." Loop control is critical to effective and precise casting. A loop describes the shape of the fly line as it rolls off the rod tip. The profile of a good loop looks like the shape of an air foil and is formed by loading and stopping the fly rod properly. Loading the rod means forcing it to bend, and the application of that force can be compared to starting and stopping a car. You accelerate slowly and smoothly and gradually apply just the right amount of power to keep the car moving at a steady speed. Abruptly stopping the rod, like slamming on the brakes, is the second essential step to forming good loops. One of the indisputable truths in fly fishing is that snapping and stopping the rod forms the loops. If you do it correctly, the motion is quick. To help you remember this concept, think of the word **SNOP!** The word is a neologism coined from the words snap and stop.

Accelerating then stopping the fly rod forms the loops.

With the line in the air, fly casting differentiates itself from other forms of fishing in that the back cast is equally, if not more, important than the forward cast because its proper execution sets up the entire casting stroke. Fly casting, with the exception of the roll cast, needs equal power in both directions. Our muscles are not accustomed to that backward movement, but to cast effectively you must develop that skill.

I had the opportunity to attend the Wulff Instructors School in 1996.

Each student was given a rod handle, and we practiced what Joan Wulff refers to as the "screendoor handle analogy." The technique emphasizes pushing the thumb forward while simultaneously pulling the fingers back. This exercise duplicates the power snap that Joan considers essential to loading and stopping the fly rod which helps form good loops. Joan calls it the "power snap." (Figure 4.3) Lefty Kreh and respected author Ed Jaworowski say, "Continuously accelerate and then stop the rod." Internationally recognized casting instructor Mel Krieger refers to it as "whu-u-ump the rod," and British author and casting champion, the late Hugh Falkus taught us to, "Snap the bloody rod in half."

I don't care what you call it, but to cast effectively, you must snap and stop the rod going back and again coming forward. I compare the casting motion to the way you would swing and stop a fly swatter, but in both directions. These controlled, precise movements that begin with the loading move and accelerate to an abrupt stop work in concert to turn over the rod tip properly and form good loops.

FIGURE 4.3

Always remember that the backward and forward stroke are a mirror image: they need to be of the same length and force and made in a straight line.

CASTING ARC

The casting arc, or casting stroke, is the measurable distance between the extremes of the backward and forward movement of the rod tip (Figure 4.4). The path of the fly rod during the cast must be maintained in a straight line, and the length of the stroke should be commensurate with the distance that needs to be covered by the amount of fly line you have in the air. In other words, short distances require a narrow casting stroke while long distances require a wider stroke.

FIGURE 4.4

To illustrate this concept, think in terms of a typical graphite fly rod divided into thirds. The tip cast uses the tip section of the rod for short distances of approximately 20 to 40 feet. The fly line should feel as though it's flicking off the top of the rod. The amount of energy and hand motion needed to accomplish a tip cast can be compared to throwing a dart. The mid-section of the rod will provide the power necessary to cast distances of approximately 40 to 50 feet. The hand motion needed to perform it would be similar to swatting a fly. The butt cast employs the powerful butt section of the rod and is capable of casting distances of 60 feet and beyond. The force needed would be similar to driving a nail. However, keep in mind that Dr. Harvey told us that most trout are caught within 35 feet, so there is no need for anyone, especially someone just starting out, to be overly concerned with long-distance casting. Author and instructor Harry Murray agrees and suggests that beginners should learn to "cast well rather than far."

The fundamentals mentioned here are prerequisites to the more advanced casting skills required in salmon, saltwater and steelhead fly fishing where casts of significantly greater distances than 35 feet are required.

I do need to point out that the angle of the casting arc must change with the conditions. This is true in all four directions: front, back, and to both sides. For example, if you have cover behind you or wind coming from the front or either side, you may need to tilt the cast. By tilting your body slightly and adjusting the angle of your arm, you can achieve a higher or lower trajectory of the fly line (Figure 4.5). Before casting, you need to take a good look around and think about what kind of cast you need to make. Author and casting expert, Professor Ed Jaworowski reminds us that "the common mistake that beginners and veterans make involves not using the most important accessory of all which sits atop our shoulders."

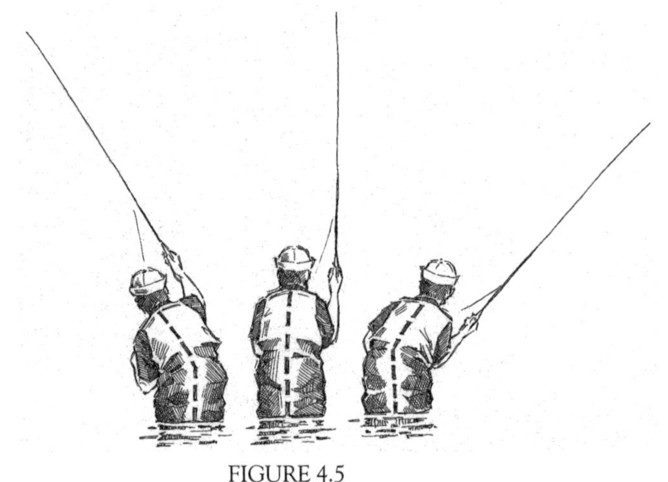

FIGURE 4.5

Again, I cannot overemphasize the importance of getting professional instruction and practicing all of the casting techniques described in this chapter.

Instructor, author and Cabela's fly fishing advisory board member Fred Arbona notes, "Throughout the past twenty-two years in the trade, beginners pass by the stage of casting much too quickly. I've seen legions of fly fishermen be frustrated, stumped or just plain give up in disgust because they never truly learned to cast well."

Fly fishing instructor and past National Coordinator of the Federation of Fly Fishers Women's Education Program Maggie Merriman tells us, "One does not learn fly fishing or any sport in just one day or on a weekend. Beginners need to set aside time to practice their casting."

A few years ago, I had the opportunity to attend the John Jacobs Golf School. One of the many lessons that I learned was that it takes at least 70 repetitions before your muscles memorize a new skill. The same principle applies to casting. Therefore, please don't become discouraged if your initial attempts aren't perfect.

DRAG

Drag is any unnatural movement of your fly and must be avoided at all cost. Leon Chandler agrees. "I believe drag is the greatest problem facing fly fishermen working in moving water," Chandler remarked.

A badly dragging dry fly (Figure 4.6) creates a surface disturbance that resembles the V-shaped wake made by the bow of a speed boat.

It is often very difficult to detect the subtle effects of drag when standing 35 feet away from your fly. Unfortunately for us, however, fish see it with uncanny ability. I've seen trout drift three or four feet down stream inspecting a dry fly only to reject it and swim away. Why didn't the fish take it? Some refusals will always remain a mystery, but one answer is that the fly was not behaving naturally. Insects are virtually weightless on or under the surface of the water. In contrast, an artificial fly is not only heavier, but it is attached to the leader and often under tension from the fly line. It is little wonder that flies drag and fish don't take them.

Drag is any unnatural movement of your fly.

FIGURE 4.6

To help avoid this problem, you must introduce "controllable slack" into your fly line and leader. Creating slack can be accomplished by learning to mend, a technique we will discuss later in this chapter, and using any of the casts mentioned in this chapter.

THE BASIC CASTS

When learning to cast, it is helpful to envision the face of a clock (Figure 4.7). Stand so that your head is at the twelve o'clock position, with your eyes facing two o'clock and your belt buckle pointing toward three o'clock.

FIGURE 4.7

Because fly casting is a compound movement of your entire arm and shoulder, you must remember two critical points. First, your hand and forearm will move back and forth from the elbow, as if you are throwing darts. Simultaneously, your elbow will lift slightly on the backcast and lower again on the forward cast, like swatting a fly or driving a nail into a wall. Regardless of the length of fly line these two independent movements work together to produce one continuous motion. This explanation may sound a little complicated, especially if you are just starting out, but read on. It will all make sense.

All casts are divided into two major categories: (1) the roll cast (with the line on the water) and (2) the pick-up and lay-down cast (with the line in the air). The basic execution for both casts is nearly identical. The only difference is the speed of the backcast. Regardless of category, every good cast starts with the proper hand position and a relaxed posture. Maintaining good posture throughout your day on stream will help you avoid muscle strain in your shoulders and back. Stand up straight and tall with your chin up, chest out and stomach held in. Lumbar-sacral supports are available at some tackle dealers or fitness supply shops. These comfortable belts will hold in your abdomen and help protect your lower back. Rodmaker, casting authority and author of *A Fly Fisher's Life,* the late Charles Ritz wrote, "When you take a rod in your hand, you must be relaxed. Proper relaxation is at least half the secret of good fly casting." This is sound advice. Your casting arm and shoulder should be relaxed and the elbow flexed at 90 degrees, resting comfortably at your side. Last, your bent wrist and forearm should point down to just above the surface of the water or ground.

Every cast must be initiated with the rod tip lowered and the slack line removed. According to Lefty Kreh, these two points are vitally important.

"The biggest mistake is elevating the fly rod tip before beginning the backcast," maintains Lefty. "Most levels of fly fishers fail to understand this principle and develop all sorts of bad loops and presentations as a result." Respected author and instructor Dave Whitlock agrees. "The problems start by . . . not beginning every cast with a low rod tip and a tight line. The 'lift' or pickup is the key to a successful . . . cast."

Regardless of the type of cast, you must remember that the fly line always follows the path of the rod tip. Wherever your rod tip stops, the line will go in that direction.

For now, think of the fly rod as an extension of your forearm. As you initiate the cast, try not to lose sight of your thumb as your hand comes up toward the side of your face. Your stance should be relaxed with your feet spread apart to shoulder width and open to the target, the foot on your casting arm side turned out slightly and placed back a few inches behind the other. Keep your knees flexed and your weight evenly distributed over both feet. Whether casting from the bank or in the water, most anglers find that turning the casting arm side of their body back approximately 20 degrees to the flow is more comfortable than standing squarely to the target or against the current.

All of the casting techniques described in this chapter are made easier when you incorporate some backward and forward body weight shift, synchronized with your casting motion. However, I must caution you to keep body motion to a minimum when you are in the water. Clumsy or unnecessary movements cause vibration and noise which frighten fish.

When practicing, everyone, but especially beginners, can learn a great deal about loading a fly rod and getting the feel of the backward and forward strokes if they turn slightly to watch the fly line straighten behind them. The best alternative would be to stand perpendicular to the water and perform a side arm cast which will allow you to watch the path of the rod and fly line. An exercise which Joan Wulff devised for this horizontal technique can be performed easily in a field and is safer without a fly attached.

To practice, simply take two brightly colored flat objects (about the size of a pie pan) and spread them 50 feet apart. Stand in between the two objects at approximately one rod length from the halfway point between them. Pull out 25 feet of fly line and cast sidearm, your palm and reel facing up. Aim your casts above the objects, allowing the fly line or leader to drop on top of them. This exercise not only develops timing, it improves accuracy and emphasizes the importance of always aiming at a target.

To develop good casting techniques you need to practice, and practice can be expedited by using only 25 to 30 feet of fly line. To get the line beyond the top of the rod tip, pull the first two or three feet of fly line through the top of the rod tip, grip the rod and lower the tip. Continue pulling line from the reel while simultaneously shaking the rod from side to side. Once the measured line is beyond the tip, tie a small piece of brightly colored yarn to the end of the tippet with an arbor knot (see footnote no. 3 on page 45) and hold the fly line under your middle finger firmly against the rod grip so no additional line can slip out.

The Roll Cast

The roll cast is the best cast to help a beginner develop the feeling of loading a fly rod. If you learn only this one cast, you can fish anywhere; however, you need to practice it on water because the friction of the fly line on the surface is necessary to load the rod. This cast cannot be done otherwise.

The roll cast is especially useful when you have thick cover at your back, preventing you from making a normal back cast. It is also valuable when straightening or repositioning the fly line prior to picking it up and making the back cast of the pick-up and lay-down technique which we will discuss next.

Remove 25 to 30 feet of fly line from your reel and work it out onto the water by lowering your rod tip and shaking the rod. The first few roll casts are always made more difficult by all the fly line piled on top of the water directly in front of you, so don't become discouraged when your initial attempts aren't perfect.

Start the roll cast by lowering the rod tip while pointing it slightly away from the casting arm side of your body (Figure 4.8). This placement will separate the rod from the path of the fly line on the backcast. Raise the rod tip and your entire bent arm slowly to the twelve o'clock

FIGURE 4.8

position while simultaneously bending your body back slightly. Allow the fly line to drape behind your casting shoulder and come to a dead stop. Your thumb should be near your forehead, with the rod tip pointed at eleven o'clock. When you are ready to initiate the cast, rock your body forward a little, lowering your bent arm and elbow, and snap your hand and rod over and forward, like swatting a fly on a wall. This will bring the rod tip to an abrupt stop at two o'clock, or eye level. Your thumb must end up parallel to the water. The fly line should roll out on or just above the water. Lower your hand and rod tip toward the water on the follow-through to finish the cast.

The three steps to perform a successful roll cast are: **1.** loading move and stop; **2.** snap; **3.** stop; and follow through.

Always remember to aim slightly to the side of the line on the water.

By that I mean in still water a right-handed caster should aim to the left of the line on the water, and a left-handed caster should aim to the right. If you don't, your rod will hit the fly line on the forward stroke. Be aware when you are on stream that the direction the water is flowing may cause you to reverse the aforementioned. This will require you to cast off your opposite shoulder. The technique can be achieved by simply lifting your hand slightly and pointing your elbow away from your shoulder similar to a military salute. The rod tip and fly line will then move over the opposite shoulder, while your casting hand stays above your eyes, allowing you to look at the target from under the rod shaft. Remember to reverse your foot position.

To lengthen the line when roll casting, simply pull some additional line from the reel and work it out on to the water prior to making another forward cast. Do not allow line to slip out prematurely on the backward stroke. Too much slack line will prevent you from loading the rod properly.

Pick-Up and Lay-Down

The second cast I want to discuss is called the pick-up and lay-down. It is the basic technique for all aerial casts and can be practiced in or out of the water. Begin by roll casting 25 to 30 feet of fly line straight out on to the water or manually placing the same in front of you on the ground. The pick-up and lay-down cast, like the roll cast, requires a relaxed arm and shoulder and a good hand position with an extended wrist, the rod tip lowered and the slack line removed.

Slowly lift the rod tip to break the surface adhesion of the water if you are practicing on water to start the end of the line moving. As soon as you see the leader move toward you, snap your hand and bent arm up, moving the rod tip to the twelve o'clock position. Then stop! This motion looks like a baseball umpire's arm when he signals an out. Keep your thumb near your forehead and along the casting arm side of your face (Figure 4.9). Momentum invariably causes the rod tip to travel back farther; however, do not cock your wrist. Standing slightly open to your target will allow you to glance back quickly to watch the fly line unroll behind you on the back cast. When the line has almost straightened (Figure 4.10) and the rod stops vibrating, rock your body forward slightly, lower your bent arm and elbow from the shoulder and snap your hand and the rod over and forward slightly to the two o'clock position and stop. Your thumb must point parallel to the water. After three or four feet of fly line has cleared the rod tip, gently lower your hand and rod tip on the follow-through to just above the water to finish the cast.

The six steps necessary to perform a successful pick-up and lay-down cast are: **1.** loading move; **2.** snap; **3.** stop; and follow through, pause -

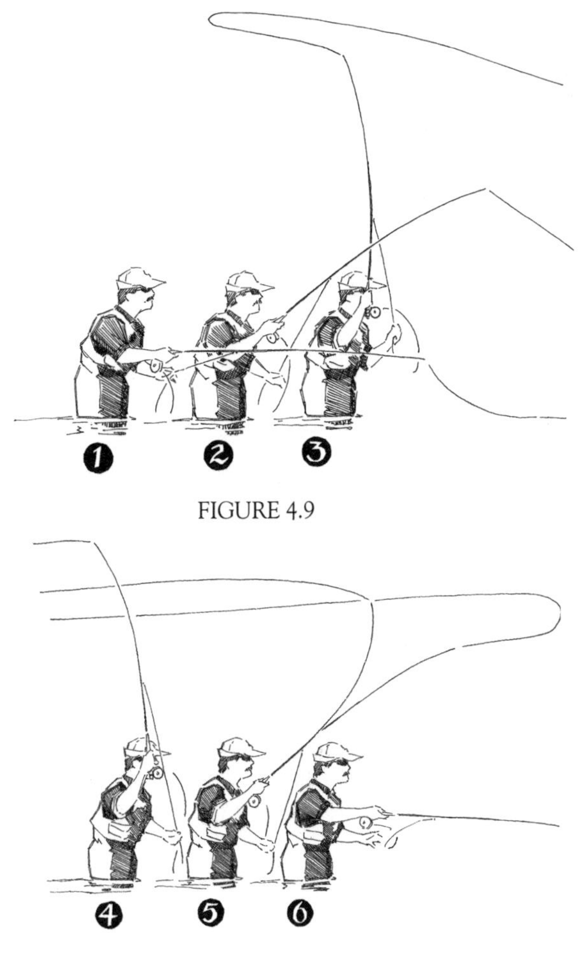

FIGURE 4.9

FIGURE 4.10

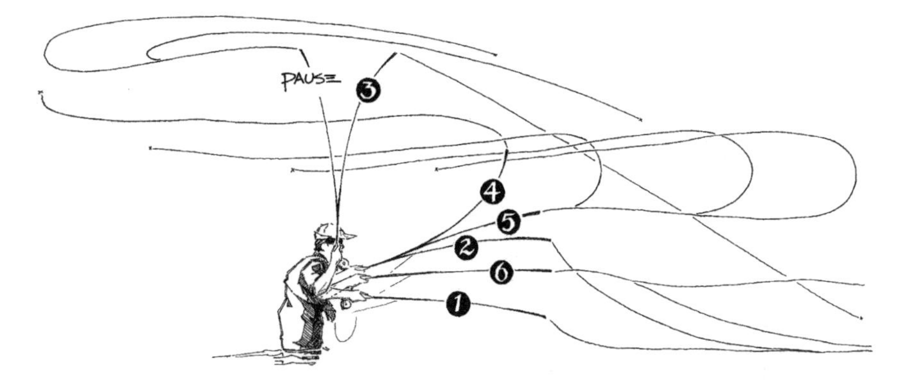

FIGURE 4.11

loading move; **4.** snap; **5.** stop; **6.** follow through (Figure 4.11). Notice, this technique is called the "pick-up", not the "pick-over". As we discussed earlier, the biggest single mistake that beginners make is cocking the wrist, causing the rod and fly line to drop back to the nine o'clock position and the line, leader and fly to slap the water or snag in the cover. Like the roll cast, the pick-up and lay-down needs to be practiced off your opposite shoulder. To recap this technique, reverse your stance and lift your hand slightly while pointing your elbow away from your shoulder. The rod tip will move above your opposite shoulder. Remember to keep your hand slightly above your eyes which will allow you to look at your target from under the rod shaft.

PAUSE

Most sports share one thing in common — follow through. Follow through is the natural extension of the swing. Fly casting is no exception, but in addition to the forward cast, the backward cast requires it, too!

Author and casting expert Al Caucci contends, "Casters have a tendency not to 'wait' on their back cast . . . not realizing that the more line they put out, the longer they must wait until the line in the back cast straightens." It has been his experience that "this is one of the bigger errors that the advanced caster makes."

I have added an additional arm position to this pick-up and lay-down casting sequence to emphasize the importance of waiting, or pausing, until the fly line straightens (Figures 4.12, 4.13).

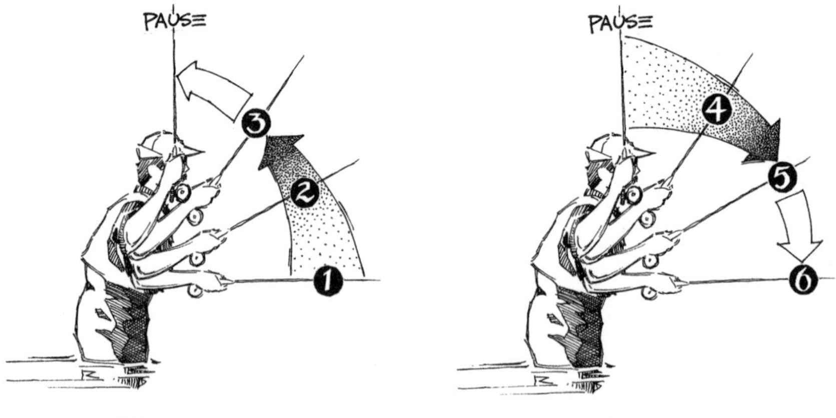

FIGURE 4.12

FIGURE 4.13

Al Caucci says, "wait." I say, "pause." Call it anything you like as long as you remember to do it every time on short casts of 30 to 40 feet.

The time that it takes for increased lengths of fly line to unroll is what Joan Wulff refers to as drift time. You must continue to follow through after the backcast stop by moving your hand up and back slightly in the same direction that the rod hand was moving before the stop. Lift your elbow but do not cock your wrist! This split second will allow you to relax momentarily, even change direction, yet keep a feeling of being connected to the fly through the tension in the line. When the rod handle quits vibrating, start the loading move of the forward cast.

This skill takes patience and time to develop because it happens so quickly and the feeling is very subtle. Like all the other fundamentals that we have discussed, this one is essential and needs to be understood and practiced.

False Cast

The next cast is a variation of the pick-up and lay-down. The false cast is a technique in which the line, leader, and fly do not drop to the water or ground before another casting cycle is initiated (Figure 4.14).

FIGURE 4.14

You need to learn to false cast for a variety of reasons. First, you can use it to lengthen or shorten the fly line. Second, the false cast lets you change direction while the line is in the air, enabling you to keep the rod, fly line, leader and their shadow from the trout's view before turning to make the final presentation to the fish. Third, the false cast allows you to dry the fly. Each time a dry fly hits the water it absorbs a bit of moisture, adding weight to the fly. This added weight causes the fly to become more susceptible to drag or sinking. Finally, when moving a few steps to a new stream position, false casting will help prevent tangles or the need to rewind most of the line. Students often ask how many times they should false cast? A good rule of thumb is to false cast the dry fly in an oblique direction a few times between presentations especially if your fly is sinking. Instructor, guide and member of the Orvis® advisory board member Lori-Ann Murphy emphasizes the point: "A common problem that beginners make is false casting too much in a fishing situation, thereby spooking fish."

Remember, when using a wet fly, nymph, or streamer under the surface, you want your fly to sink quickly, so keep your false casting in this situation to a minimum to avoid drying it.

YOUR LINE HAND – SHOOTING LINE

Until now all your practice should have been accomplished with the fly line held firmly against the rod grip. Now it's time to learn to use your line hand.

The line hand is used to pull fly line from the reel and also retrieve it while fishing. In addition to those important functions, the line hand is used to control the length of the fly line and maintain tension on it which helps to load the rod. Last, the line hand releases the extra line on the final presentation stroke, allowing the reserve to shoot through the guides, extending the cast.

FIGURE 4.15

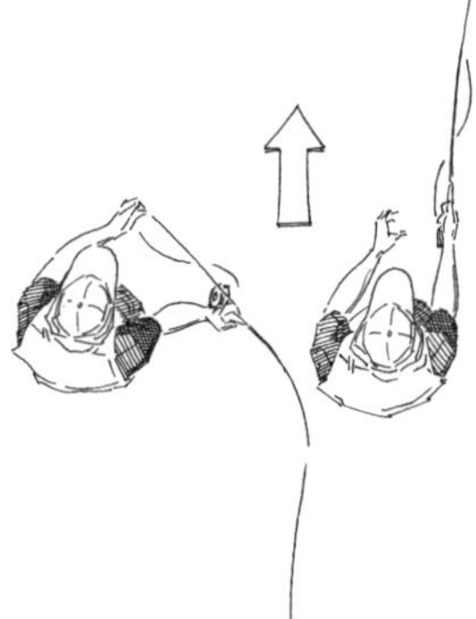

Prior to starting a pick-up and lay-down cast, it is a good practice to pull a few extra feet of fly line from the reel. Pinch the line firmly between the thumb and index finger of your line hand at the first stripping guide. Simultaneously pull in the slack, lower the rod tip, and hold your line hand comfortably at your side. Repeat this step as often as necessary until all the slack is gone.

Once the slack is removed you can initiate the cast of your choice. During the pick-up and lay-down cast, your line hand should flex up and down in sync with your rod hand's movement. This will maintain a consistent length of line and load the rod equally on the backward and forward strokes. Be careful not to allow any line to slip out on the back cast or the timing may be off, making it difficult to load the rod and present the fly properly. As you look to your target, estimate its distance from you and pull out the amount of fly line that you think you will need to reach it. Start casting and when you are confident that the length of line you have in the air and in reserve is right, begin your final presentation stroke. As that stroke ends, abruptly stop the rod at eye level, 2 o'clock, and let go of the line (Figure 4.15). The fly line should shoot through the guides and out the tip top. Follow through by gently lowering your hand and the rod tip, allowing the fly line to settle on the water or ground.

Remember that even a poorly executed cast can catch a trout. Therefore, you should be ready to catch a fish each and every time your fly lands on the water. Point your rod in the direction of the fly with your rod hand. Strip in the slack with your line hand, which we'll discuss next, and continually turn your body and the rod to follow the drift of the fly throughout its entire swing.

STRIPPING LINE

At the completion of the cast it is necessary to minimize the slack that accumulated in the line during the drift of the line and fly, otherwise you run the risk of your fly dragging prematurely. To correctly strip in line, immediately take the line from your line hand as the fly lands on the water and tuck it under the relaxed middle finger of your rod hand (Figure 4.16). In essence, your finger becomes another stripping guide. Simply point and follow the fly with your rod tip and body, stripping in line from behind your rod hand. This procedure puts the fly and line under your immediate control, and you will then be ready to tighten your fingers on the grip and set the hook when a strike occurs.

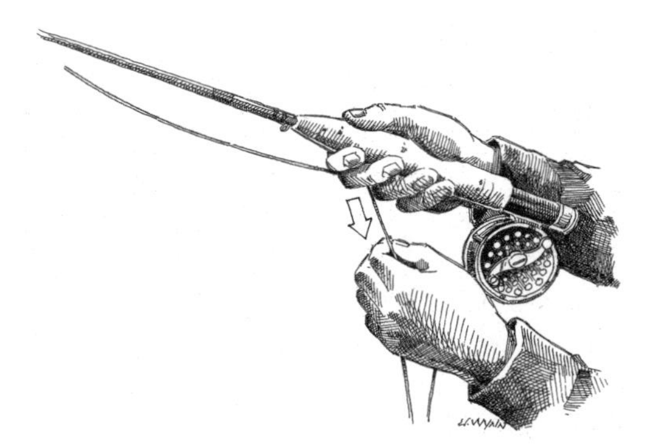

FIGURE 4.16

PRESENTATION CASTS AND ADVANCED TECHNIQUES

The fly is not cast directly to the fish; the fly is cast upstream ahead of the fish, letting the current present it to the trout as naturally as possible. A straight line cast is extremely accurate and often used in windy conditions or when fishing with wet flies and streamers. In a straight line cast the fly line is tight to the rod, meaning there is no slack in the line or leader. No slack in the line produces immediate control of the fly and retrieve. However, when fishing in moving water, you may want to have some controllable slack in your line to help eliminate drag in order to take some pressure off the fly. This slack allows a wet fly or streamer to sink more quickly, or a dry fly to float longer naturally, making a more realistic presentation to the fish.

The Bounce Cast

The bounce cast can be performed by simply adding power to the final presentation stroke in the pick-up and lay-down casting technique mentioned on pages 68-70. Abruptly stop the rod tip at the one o'clock position without letting any additional line slip out. The resulting vibration will bounce the line back toward you as you simultaneously lower your hand and rod tip toward the water. You will immediately notice the controllable slack that has been introduced into the fly line as it lies on the surface of the water. A variation of the bounce cast can be performed by snapping the line back in your line hand simultaneously as the rod stops and the fly is presented to the water. Unfortunately, distance will be lost with these two techniques. To compensate for it, lengthen the line when false casting before you make the presentation.

The Reach Cast

I consider any upstream cast to be very effective because it offers the best hooking angle of the fly, but dropping the leader and line directly over a trout could frighten it because of the resulting splash or shadow. As you advance in your casting ability, you can avoid this situation by aiming to the side of the fish and using the reach cast.

Popularized by Doug Swisher and Dr. Carl Richards, this cast, also referred to as an aerial mend, will help keep the line and leader from landing on top of a trout. As I mentioned earlier in this chapter, the fly line will always follow the path of the rod tip. To introduce controllable slack into the line, you can, on the presentation stroke, point the rod tip in the direction of your target and abruptly stop the rod. As the line straightens in front of you, reach across your body in either direction with your rod hand and release the reserve line from your line hand (Figure 4.17). Finish the cast by immediately returning the rod to the front position, lower the tip and tuck the fly line under the relaxed middle finger of your rod hand. You will see a curve of slack line fall on the water in the direction of the reach. Though this curve will be moved by the current, it won't allow your tippet to be adversely affected or the fly to drag until the line finally straightens out. This technique is one of the most important presentation casts for everyone to learn.

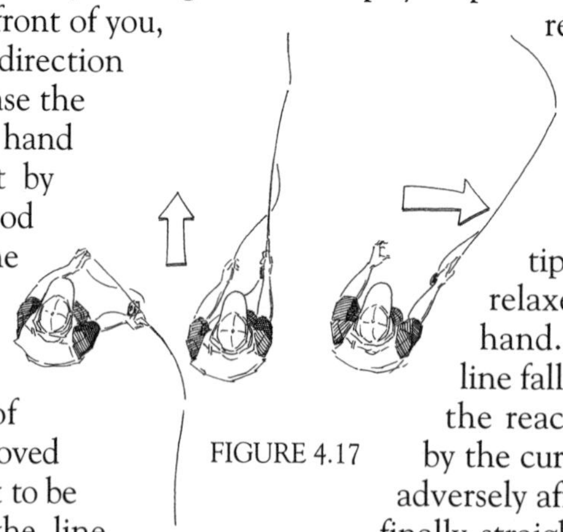

FIGURE 4.17

FIGURE 4.18

The Wiggle Cast

One of the most useful slack line casts that is also fun to do is the "wiggle cast." The wiggle cast is a variation of the pick-up and lay-down. This cast is performed by shaking the rod grip from side to side at the conclusion of the presentation stroke. Wiggling the grip imparts vibration to the tip, causing the line to be presented to the water in multiple "S" curves (Figure 4.18). These curves absorb drag as they straighten. Unlike the straight line presentation of the pick-up and lay-down technique, the wiggle cast will be far less affected by the varying currents. The wiggle cast gives the fly a long, drag-free float, resulting in a more natural presentation to the waiting trout. It is especially useful for downstream presentation where the current will straighten the "S" curves before dragging the fly. The wiggle cast also shortens the casting distance, requiring some compensation in line length.

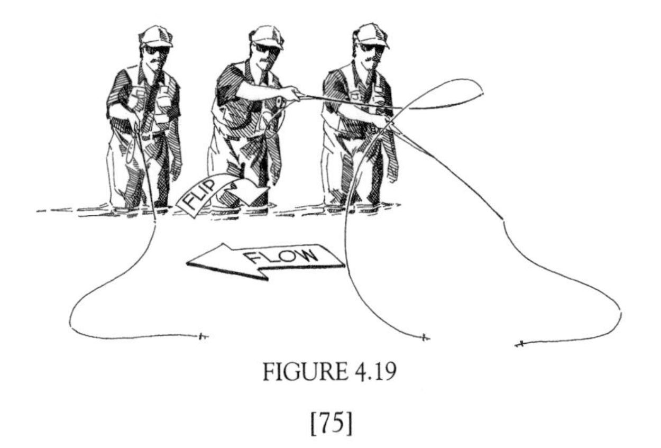

FIGURE 4.19

Mending

Mending adds controllable slack to a fly line that is already on the water. This technique moves the line in front of the rod, taking pressure off the fly, thus allowing a wet fly or streamer to sink faster or a dry fly to float drag-free longer. It is accomplished by flipping the rod and line with a straight arm in a semicircular motion upstream (Figure 4.19). Keep in mind that the flipping should be done with a minimal disturbance of the water. Perform this as often as you are able or deem necessary throughout the entire drift of the fly. Make sure the fly line stays upstream of a dry fly on the water. For a mend to be most effective, it should reach all the way out to the leader.

Roll Cast Pick-Up

The roll cast can also be incorporated into what is called the "roll cast pick-up." This technique is an efficient, effective and quiet way to get the fly and line off the water and into the air. It is accomplished by doing a roll cast but not allowing the line and fly to hit the water at the conclusion of the presentation stroke. Once the fly line starts to roll away from the rod tip and is nearly straight, do not allow it to drop. Keep the rod and line up by immediately starting the back cast of the pick-up and lay-down technique.

Single Haul Pick-Up

Another technique that quickly and quietly gets your fly and line off the water and back into the air is the single haul pick-up. It is accomplished by pulling the line away from your body with your line hand and removing any slack while simultaneously lifting and snapping the rod into the pick-up and lay-down backcast position. This technique will delicately lift the fly from the water and allow you to start casting again without stripping in most of the fly line.

A FINAL THOUGHT

Being flexible and creative is vitally important to successful fly fishing. Acquiring additional skills, including curve casts, single and double hauls and other advanced techniques, will refine the sport for you. For example, a narrow cushion of calm air lies between the surface of the water and the wind above it. On extremely blustery days, a side-arm cast is most useful to get under the wind and present the fly.

Nationally recognized instructors Barry and Cathy Beck contend that, "being self-taught is the biggest mistake a beginner can make;" the second according to respected author and instructor Dave Whitlock, would be, "having a spouse, parent or neighbor teach you how to fish!"

Another reason why some fishermen don't succeed is that they are afraid to fail. My advice, especially to the beginner, is to attend a quality casting school and then get out and fish. Mel Krieger contends that "the quintessence of learning is doing." You will make mistakes, but each one of them will be a valuable lesson. Practice, observation and self-analysis will help you build skills. Fly fishing expert George Anderson reminds everyone, veterans included, to, "get professional help when you get in a rut. Many anglers plug away making the same basic mistakes. Hire a good teaching guide for a day and let the pro tune-up everything from casting to fishing techniques." When you seek professional instruction or employ a fishing guide, I can assure you the experience will be far more pleasant and productive if you listen to what they suggest and then practice what you have learned.

Remember the following advice: practice pays; seek professional help, especially if you are having a problem; and never become discouraged.

WYNN

AMERICA'S FIRST LADY OF FLY FISHING

Joan not only embodies the strength and excellence we strive for, but in doing so she doesn't lose the grace and sensitivity of the woman she is. The blend of her strength and femininity parallels the marriage of casting and fishing . . . we will always look up to her.

– P. Woolley

For years, Rich and Earl had been inviting me to go fly fishing with them in Montana. "Come on, Tom," they'd say, "we'll spend three days on Nelson's and DePuy's spring creeks, then go over to fish the Big Horn. You'll love it!" Unfortunately, my business responsibilities, as well as the close proximity on the calendar to our yearly hunting trip, kept me from going.

The year 1995 was different, and although I wasn't going with Rich and Earl, Sara my fiancée at the time and I were able to get time off and purchase tickets to Montana. As a bonus, my friend Tom Mikunda would be our host. Tom said that we could use his McKenzie drift boat, and he'd even be our guide. I was so excited that just the thought of going had me smiling from ear to ear. Unfortunately, within weeks of our trip Sara changed her mind. She wanted to go to a golf school instead. After a day spent sulking, I set about cancelling all of our reservations. Now the real work began! Where was I going to find a reasonably priced, quality golf school at the eleventh hour?

Lady luck smiled down on us. I was able to book a week at the Hanah Resort in Margaretville, New York, home to the John Jacobs Golf School and only an eight-hour drive from Pittsburgh. Talk about more good fortune, the east branch of the Delaware River ran right through the golf course, and the famous Esopus, Beaverkill, and Willowemoc trout streams were only a short drive away. But even that wasn't the best of it!

We were going to meet Mrs. Joan Wulff at her Lew Beach home just outside of Roscoe. I am continually amazed at how the mind forms a picture of someone before we have met them. All I knew about Joan was what I had read about her and the impressions I formed from our recent phone conversations.

Joan Salvato Wulff was born in 1926 and raised in a suburb of Paterson, New Jersey. Her father, Jimmy Salvato, owned a sporting goods shop, wrote the outdoor column for the *Paterson Morning Call,* and frequented the local casting club. Although members brought their sons to the club, little thought was given to bringing along a daughter. When Jimmy finally invited Joan to accompany him, that was the beginning of her love affair with fly fishing. In 1937 at the age of eleven she won her first casting competition and now holds a total of 18 national and international titles. Joan also established the women's distance casting record of 161 feet.

When the morning of our visit finally arrived, Sara and I stopped at a bakery to purchase some goodies before heading south. The view of the Catskill Mountains that we saw as we traveled was breathtaking. Following Joan's directions, we turned left off Barkaboom Road and the upper Beaverkill River came into full view. Our landmark was a stone wall with a black mailbox, and within moments we spotted the white frame house nestled on the mountain slope. The gravel crunched under our tires as we turned onto the driveway and wound our way up the hill and through her property. We passed by her son's home, two casting ponds, the school building, a cottage, and finally arrived at the parking lot. Almost immediately I was out of the car and at the back door of the home. I could see Mrs. Wulff standing in the kitchen.

As I stood on the porch, I was struck by the woman's stately appearance and how gracefully she moved around the room. I knocked on the door. "Come in," she called. I could tell by the warmth of her welcome that she liked people. Why else would a single woman receive two strangers into her home? Her handshake was confident and strong, and after we exchanged greetings and introductions, Joan went back to preparing coffee, tea, and cookies for the three of us.

Her home reflected her love of the sport. The upper portion of two walls in the great room were tastefully decorated with sporting prints of every description. One of these walls was lined half way to the ceiling with bookshelves filled to overflowing; the opposite wall held an entertainment center. Classical music played softly in the background and Joan explained that dancing was her other passion. Unfortunately, she did not have enough time for it. "I am convinced that the dancing lessons improved my casting because they taught me to use my entire body," Joan told us. An imposing floor-to-ceiling stone fireplace occupied another wall in the great room while the opposite wall had a bank of windows that overlooked the magnificent grounds. We could see the Beaverkill River in the valley and the Catskill Mountains rising in the distance.

I asked Joan how she came to live in such a wonderful place. She explained that she and her late husband Lee were invited to speak at the 1977 Federation of Fly Fishers conclave in Roscoe. When they saw the beauty of the region, they both knew it was the perfect place for a fishing school. "There were fishermen everywhere, and the rivers were full of trout," she remarked. The Wulff's moved to Roscoe the following spring.

The custom made breakfront provided the great room's focal point, dividing the kitchen from the rest of the room. The entire space atop it was devoted to the well-deserved trophies and awards that the Wulffs have received over the years. I was most impressed with the Angler of the Year award given to Joan in 1994 by *Fly Rod & Reel Magazine*.

Joan met Lee Wulff while she was filming a bluefin tuna segment for ABC's "American Sportsman" series. At the time they both worked for the Garcia Corporation. She has traveled and fished throughout the world and seems to enjoy tarpon and salmon fishing above all others. "There is just something special about catching large fish on light tackle," she said. It dawned on me that in a male-dominated sport, Joan must have felt as though she was living in the shadow of one of fly fishing's icons being married to Lee. The Wulffs were the royal couple of the sport, and as a team the two profoundly influenced the fly fishing world. Lee passed away in 1991, and I assumed his death must have left a large void in her life. When I asked her about it, Joan was candid: "If Lee had died fifteen years ago, I don't know what I would have done. After all, my life was taken over by him. He was an exceptional man, and living in a remote place like this, you end up out-of-touch a lot. However, when I wrote my books and kept the schools going, I became more confident in my own ability." She estimated that the couple taught over 2,000 students since the school opened in 1979.

Joan asked if we wanted more coffee, and I offered to get the pot. When I came back to the porch, Joan was showing Sara the mechanics of the cast without the use of a rod. The coordinated movements of her arm were precise, and I was struck by how expressively she used her opposite hand to point out every detail. She accompanied the demonstration with a passionate explanation that showed extraordinary insight and expertise.

Consistency seems to be the hallmark of Joan's teaching techniques, and all five instructors at the Wulff School reflect her philosophy. Joan told us that she "runs a tight ship" and takes her instructional responsibilities seriously. Nothing competes with her devotion to the school. In fact, she mentioned that in the few free moments she gets between projects, her thoughts turn to teaching.

Joan's goal is to constantly develop and improve her staff's teaching and communication skills. The Wulff's created a standard against which all others are measured. The school makes it possible for the average person to become accomplished in three days of comprehensive instruction. Joan also mentioned that she rarely teaches a "women only" school because she said she enjoys the interaction of both men and women. "If men do not understand something, they often bluff their way through, where women, on the other hand, tend to freeze up," she said. I got the distinct impression that she has sympathy for the women who attend her school, and rightfully so. All of her students are videotaped, and the students critique one another.

She would like to be remembered as the first person to analyze the mechanics of casting, and her book, *Joan Wulff's Fly Casting Techniques,* is a masterful treatise on the subject. "The book was my first contribution to the world in terms of anything," she said proudly. "That was the first thing that I ever created." Joan broke ground as the first person, male or female, to write a casting column in a national publication. "The deadlines were difficult," she said, especially with her demanding personal schedule which included raising two sons. But the discipline of writing helped her to understand the complex subject of fly casting better. She is convinced that a comfortable grip and a balanced rod, reel, and fly line combination are the most important pieces of tackle that anyone will own, especially a woman. Unfortunately, most manufacturers don't have equipment designed specifically for women. Joan thought out loud, "How nice it would be to form a study group to brainstorm designs for a woman's special [fishing] needs."

In addition to running the school, she keeps her plate heaped with projects and she redefines the adage "busy as a bee." Joan serves as vice president of the Catskill Fly Fishing Center and Museum and is currently working on the Lee Wulff Atlantic Salmon Exhibit. In 1981 the Wulffs became instrumental in establishing the center. She also writes a monthly instructional article for *Fly Rod & Reel Magazine,* advises the R. L. Winston Rod Company, and is currently working on a new book and video.[11]

At the time of our visit she had just returned from an out-of-state fly fishing school and was preparing to leave mid-week to salmon fish on the Miramichi River. I asked her if she has any hobbies outside of fishing. "I don't have time for any," she remarked. She is continually bombarded with requests for her time: to edit manuscripts, autograph and inscribe books, send out photographs, write articles, and attend meetings and speaking engagements. According to Joan, a typical day in her life is "busy from morning 'til night." I asked her where her favorite place to fish is outside of the Catskills, and she replied, "Wherever I am, I fall in love with a new river each year."

Undoubtedly, Joan Wulff has done more for women in the sport of

11. Joan Wulff's new book *Fly Casting Accuracy,* and her latest video, *Joan Wulff's Dynamics of Fly Casting,* are available from Royal Wulff Products at 914-439-4060.

fly fishing than any other person who has come before her. As she thoughtfully inscribed one of her books for us, Joan mentioned that she considers herself "an ordinary woman who has had an extraordinary life through the magic of sport fishing." With her gracious thought still lingering in the air, we rose to leave. Time is the enemy of enjoyment.

"Joanie," as she is affectionately referred to by her friends, escorted us to our car. Sara asked if I could take a picture of the two of them with the Catskill mountains in the background, and Joan obliged. As I looked through the viewfinder, I couldn't help but think what a gracious and lovely lady Mrs. Wulff is and what a beautiful place she calls "home."

Chapter Five

Entomology

Angling is the way to round out a happy life. There is romance in the knowledge that the naturals and the imitations are the same today as they were yesterday.

– Charles K. Fox

Eight years ago I took some students to Spruce Creek, and I asked them to stand behind me on the bank while I demonstrated a few casting techniques. Suddenly, a handful of sulphur mayflies started to hatch, and within moments the water surface became a blizzard of insect activity. I turned around quickly to explain what was happening and discovered all five students, hands cupped around their eyes, staring straight up at the sky. "What are you looking at?" I shouted over the sound of the rushing water. "We are trying to see where all those bugs are coming from," one man yelled in reply.

Obviously, those beginners didn't know that those stream-born sulphur mayflies were hatching on the surface of the stream and flying away, not hatching in the air and falling down on the water. Most aquatic insects must shed their immature shuck and emerge as a winged adult. This transformation is referred to as a hatch, and should not be confused with a mating swarm that occurs over the water in the air.

Insects, both aquatic (stream born) (Figure 5.1), and terrestrial (land born), make up the primary diet of trout, and the scientific study of these invertebrates is called entomology. Author and fishing expert Dr. Carl Richards believes that one of the biggest mistakes that the beginner makes is "to not know the insects which are emerging so they can pick the correct fly." If you want to be a savvy angler, you must learn to recognize the basic insect groups significant to trout fishing. Anglers have many ways to find out what insect activity is occurring on the stream they intend to visit. Some of these methods include word of

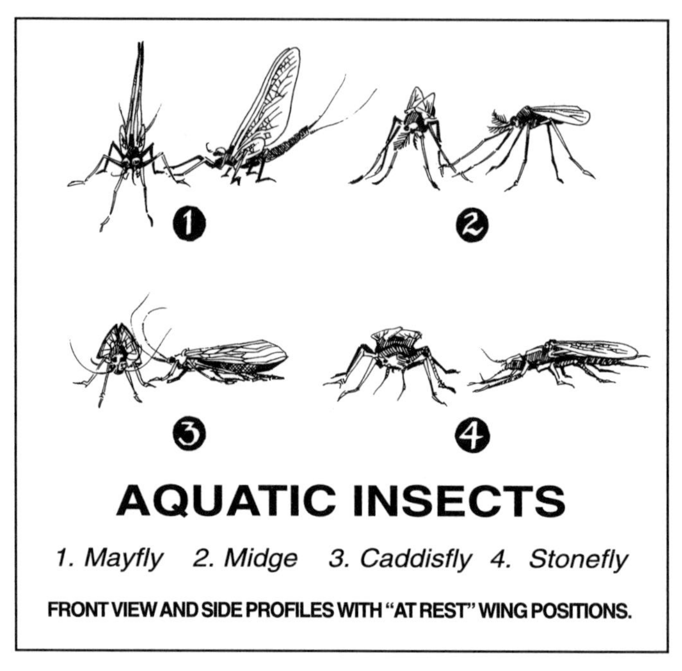

FIGURE 5.1

mouth, hatch charts, the CD-Rom program Flybase® for Windows, research books, the World Wide Web[12], contact with the fly shop that monitors the local stream, and their own eyes once they get there. The ability to understand and differentiate between the wide variety of insects is important to the intelligent and successful fly fisherman.

The following five groups of insects are most important to the trout, and thus the fly fisherman. I've also included an explanation of the typical life cycle of each.

Terrestrials

The word terrestrial is derived from the Latin "terra" which means land, ground, or earth. Terrestrials, such as beetles, ants, and grasshoppers, differ from the other four aquatic insect orders in that they are born on land and do not develop in a trout stream. However, they often land on or fall into the water accidentally and with some frequency. A cricket or beetle can be blown into the water from tall grass or tree branches by a gust of wind, for example. Cold air temperatures, which slow down an insect's level of activity, may cause an ant or grasshopper

12. The internet is an important source of information regarding all of trout fishing. The web site-address for Trout Unlimited is http://www.tu.org/trout and the address for the Federation of Fly Fishers is http://www.fedflyfishers.org.

to inadvertently topple into the water from a nearby rock.

These insects have no aquatic life cycle, but they do have four stages of development. For our purposes, the adult stage is the only one of importance to fly fisherman. Terrestrials are most active in the summer when temperatures are warm. During this period trout love to feed on them and will often travel three or four feet to devour one. To the trout, terrestrials represent a singularly attractive, protein-rich, easily obtainable meal, so the fish will expend more energy to pursue them. Larger terrestrials, such as grasshoppers, caterpillars, and cicadas, are even more appealing. Angling expert Doug Swisher calls this the "Pounds Expended Theory." In other words, the bigger the meal, the farther the fish will travel to eat it!

Adult terrestrial and a dry fly imitation.

Fly patterns that imitate terrestrials are often cast so they intentionally plop onto the water, creating a disturbance on the surface. Once the fly is on the water, the fisherman may choose to either float the fly directly on top of the water or in the surface film just beneath the surface. Because of the trout's interest in terrestrials and the clumsy way in which these insects behave in the water, be prepared to catch a fish every time your terrestrial imitation hits the water. Trout will strike when the fly is dead-drifted or twitched, or even on a dragging swing or retrieve.

Patterns that work well during warm weather months include beetles in sizes 12-18 with bodies constructed of either foam[13], cork, or deerhair in colors of black, brown, tan, rust, green, or greenish yellow. Foam or deerhair ants in sizes 12-24 also work well, and the McMurray ant, in either black or red, is tough to beat. Crickets in sizes 10-14, colored traditionally black or brown and constructed with closed cell foam bodies, can be successfully fished near banks with high grassy weeds. In the hot, humid "dog days" of summer, a yellow deerhair grasshopper, sizes 8-14, slapped down near a grassy bank and twitched somewhat to imitate a panicked insect can bring a ferocious strike from leviathan-sized trout. Other terrestrial patterns you might want to keep in your fly box should include a variety of small leafhoppers, jassids, and in the earlier warm weather, the lime green inchworm.

MIDGES

Midges are among the smallest insects that trout feed on, and they are found in nearly all streams. These diminutive insects are very hardy and

13. The John Steinhart foam beetle, as well as his ant, grasshopper, and caterpillar imitations are extremely durable and as productive a fly as you will ever use. These flies are available by phoning (412) 344-8888.

thrive in stagnant as well as moving water. They encompass a wide range of tiny flying insects with an even broader spectrum of body colors.

Born in water, midges hatch from eggs into tiny wormlike larvae. Larvae pupate under water, pupae swim to the surface, and winged adults emerge on the surface (Figure 5.2).

These mosquito-like insects literally blanket the water near the edge of converging currents, forming a feeding lane that dissipates as the faster moving water slowly ebbs into the quiet of a pool. Using a slow, cautious approach, you may notice one or several trout rhythmically sipping something from the top of the water. These fish do not seem to be in any hurry to feed, as they appear to be resting just under the surface, lazily drifting to the top of the water to sip and then slowly returning to their lie. This behavior most likely indicates that they are feeding on the midge larva or pupa trapped in the surface film.

Adult midge and a dry fly imitation.

Normally found from late February through October, midges hatch in winter, too, especially on sunny days when the temperatures are mild. Adult midges struggle to hatch, and when they do, they often hover just above the water's surface, almost daring trout to rise. At this stage they are of little interest to fish or fishermen. However, trout will rise to take them on the surface even though you might wonder why a big fish would have an appetite for such a small meal. Because midges are in such abundance, it takes very little energy for the fish to feed on them. In addition, they are often the only fish food available at the time. Remember, trout are opportunists!

Midge patterns can vary greatly, but all follow one universal rule: the imitation must be small and without tails. The Griffith's Gnat, sizes 20-26, is a good choice to have with you at all times, but the pattern choice is not as important as the presentation.

Fishing for "midging" trout represents a challenging experience, especially for the beginner. Midge-feeding trout are usually found in a narrow feeding lane just under the surface in a calm pool, or tight along the bank closely inspecting the food floating over them. Any sudden splash or motion that would disturb the serenity of the moment typically sends the fish scurrying for cover. Therefore, the cast needs to be both delicate and precise. Once a beginner has the casting techniques under control, he or she should try midge fishing. It is a shame that many anglers avoid midge fishing because of the small size of the fly and the fine tippet necessary to effectively present such a small imitation.

Because the midge imitation's size often makes it invisible on the water, the fisherman must be alert to the slightest movement on the

FIGURE 5.2

surface near the leader which may indicate a fish's strike. Even the most experienced angler can lose sight of this tiny fly. To stay connected, look past the end of the fly line to the floating leader and estimate the fly's location. Set the hook by lifting your rod gently, but deliberately, at any surface disturbance near your fly. If there is no indication of a hook-up, make sure you allow the fly to pass well behind the fish before you pick it up to recast.

CADDISFLIES

Caddisflies are aquatic insects, and trout will feed on them during most stages of their development. When the larva hatches from the egg, it resembles a small segmented worm with a head capsule. The larva attaches itself to the rocks on the bottom of the stream, and as it does, it builds a protective covering around itself, usually out of sand, gravel, or vegetative debris. Old-timers call some caddisfly larvae stickworms, as many build their protective outer cases of wood fibers, making a stick house to conceal themselves. Encased caddisfly larvae can be found by turning over the rocks submerged in the stream. Look for the cylindrical or rectangular-shaped wooden cases, or for an elongated cluster of very fine sand or gravel. After the larva pupates, it swims out of its protective case, and through the aid of gasses trapped inside its body, the pupa moves toward the water's surface (Figure 5.3). As with many species in the food chain, the caddisfly pupae have the protective coloring of their surroundings and are usually found in a range of greens, browns, and tans.

Subsurface fishing with an imitation of a caddisfly larva or pupa can be productive and should be done with a dead-drift fishing technique, letting the imitation go deep. Using a strike indicator[14] on the leader will make it easier to see a strike. When a caddisfly pupa crawls out of its protective case and makes its voyage to the top of the water, trout will feed on it at the surface, often in a "porpoise-like" fashion with the back and dorsal fin successively breaking the water's surface. Wet fly imitations, like the LaFontaine emerger, are a good choice and should be fished with a long, drag-free drift. However, let the fly drift downstream to the end of the full swing to imitate the emerger approaching the top of the water. Often the take is at the very end of the full swing.

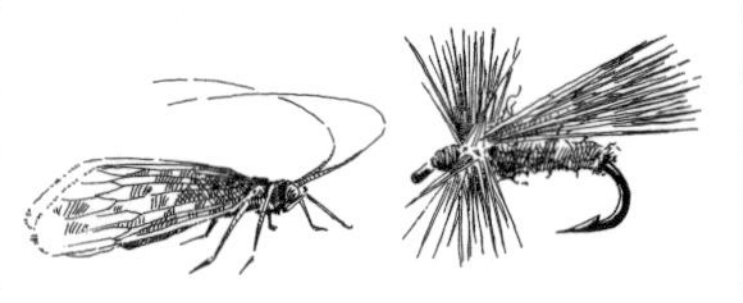

Adult caddisfly and a dry fly imitation.

Other good emerger imitations include the soft hackle and sparkle pupa, as well as traditional winged wet flies. Once again, the colors are very earthy, with browns and olive greens typically in the majority, and sizes range from 12-18, so make sure that your fly box is well stocked.

The final stage of caddisfly development is the winged adult. Trout will feed on them as they flutter their wings prior to takeoff and also when the adult female returns to deposit her eggs in the water. Adult caddisflies are recognizable by their erratic flight patterns, as well as the quick dipping and hopping motion, up and down, made on the water's surface when the female deposits her eggs. Because caddisflies are such strong fliers, they are capable of lifting off the water quickly. Trout often slash at the adult even to the point of uncharacteristically leaping out of the water as the insect tries to escape the surface. Adult caddisflies can drive fish crazy as they hover and dance over the water, landing to rest a moment, and then quickly lifting off again.

Another distinguishing feature of the adult is its two sets of wings.

14. Strike indicators are small (the approximate size of a pencil eraser), highly visible foam or cork bobbers that attach to your leader and float above the submerged fly. It will stop and/or "twitch" in the water when a fish has taken your fly just like a traditional plastic bobber.

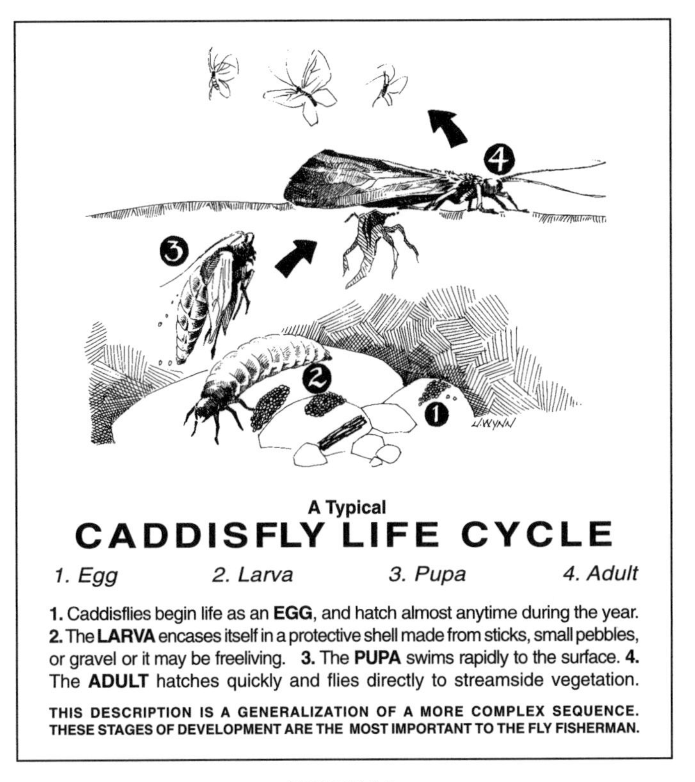

FIGURE 5.3

When the insect is at rest, the wings are folded over its abdomen forming a silhouette similar to a pup tent. Caddisflies, like midges, do not have tails and neither should your imitation.

Adult caddisflies come in a multitude of sizes and colors. Effective top water dry-fly imitations include the hairwing patterns, such as the fluttering or Elk Hair caddis, as well as the quill wing patterns, like the Henryville Special. Stiff hackle, tied palmer style, (wound over the body) will help the imitation float better. A hatch chart and color identification guide are valuable in choosing the proper pattern. However, as adult caddisflies are in the air almost all of the time, you need not be in the middle of a good caddisfly hatch to be fishing with a dry fly imitation.

STONEFLIES

According to nationally recognized author and Pennsylvania State University entomologist Greg Hoover, "Stoneflies are the herald of clean water. If your home water or the stream you plan on visiting has a healthy stonefly population, you can be assured that the water is pristine."

Stoneflies live in the fast-water stretches of many streams, with some species spending as long as three years in the nymph stage. They flourish in streams that have a rocky bottom, and they require clear, unpolluted, highly oxygenated water to thrive. Because of these requirements, stoneflies are seldom found in marginal quality water in quantities sufficient enough to be of interest to the fly fisherman. Only in rare instances, especially in the eastern United States, would an angler encounter a fishable hatch, let alone a predictable one. However, since a few species of stonefly nymphs and adults are active throughout the year, trout can still be alert to a well-presented imitation.

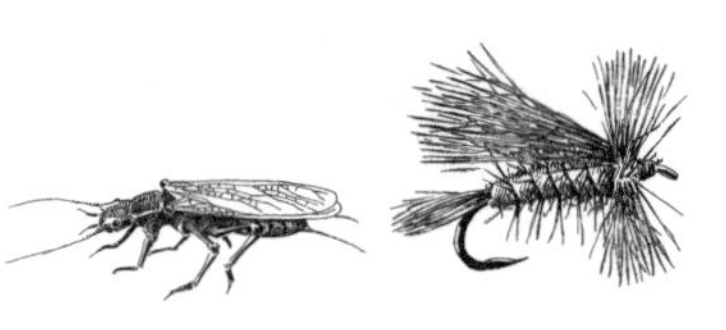

Adult stonefly and a dry fly imitation.

Stonefly adults come in a wide range of sizes. Eastern species tend to be smaller than their western cousins, but they do share a few things in common. First, a stonefly's wings, when at rest, lie flat on top of its abdomen. Second, stoneflies are clumsy flyers, occasionally striking fishermen at night or crash landing into the water. Stonefly hatches often occur early in the season and are especially prevalent in freestone streams.

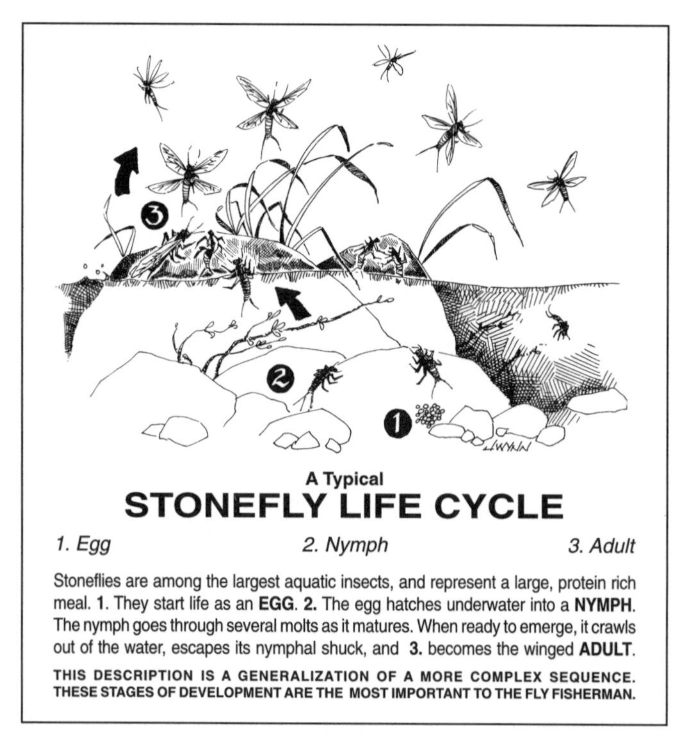

FIGURE 5.4

The little black and little yellow stonefly imitations in sizes 14-18 work well in the East for the dry fly, while weighted stoneflies in sizes 12-14 suffice for the nymphs. The salmonfly and golden stonefly in both dry fly and weighted nymph patterns are excellent choices for use in the West. Stoneflies usually crawl out of the water to emerge, *en masse*, on rocks or streamside vegetation. It is a good idea to fish your stonefly imitation near any obstruction protruding from the water and especially along the edge close to banks (Figure 5.4).

Many streams in the West, for example the Madison in Montana, the Gunnison in Colorado, and the Deschutes in Oregon, are excellent stonefly fisheries. Midwestern rivers like the Au Sable in Michigan and the Namekagon in Wisconsin have healthy populations of stoneflies too. Editor, and respected fly fishing instructor, George L. Kesel pointed out, "The Contoocook, Connecticut, Saco and Androscoggin Rivers in New Hampshire, as well as many of the lesser known streams throughout New England have abundant stonefly populations." If any of these destinations are in your fly fishing travel plans, stash away lots of stonefly patterns in your fly box. Not only will you experience excellent top-water dry fly fishing, but on many occasions a weighted stonefly nymph fished under the surface will entice a larger trout to strike.

MAYFLIES

The last group of aquatic insects are the abundant, highly-recognizable and handsomely-colored mayflies. This order constitutes virtually all the well-known hatches throughout America, and like caddisflies, they too have an aquatic life cycle and share nearly the same stages of development (Figure 5.5).

Once you discover the nymph or emerger patterns that are most productive, you can fish them identically to their caddisfly counterparts.

One of the biggest differences between mayflies and all other aquatic insects is the adult's physical appearance. As it rests on the water's surface, the wings of the adult stand upright. These newly-formed wings must dry before the insect can fly. As the adults emerge from their nymphal shucks (protective exoskeleton), the hatch is in progress, and the newly emerging adults resemble a flotilla of miniature sailboats on the water. While its wings are drying the adult mayfly is extremely vulnerable because it cannot fly. In an effort to speed up the drying process, it flutters its wings often, attracting the attention of the fish. Trout feed on the newly-hatching mayflies with a deliberate take, their snouts coming out of the water to suck the mayfly directly into their

Adult mayfly and a dry fly imitation.

mouths. Characteristically, there is a well-defined ring and bubble left on the surface of the water after the trout has risen and taken the fly.

To fish the adult mayfly pattern you should cast your fly upstream seeking the longest drag-free float possible. As soon as the fly drags, pick up your line and cast again. Drag is a dead giveaway that your fly is not behaving like the real insect, and this usually warns the wary trout that your offering is not natural.

After hatching and successfully lifting off the water to land in streamside vegetation, mayflies molt one more time (usually within a day of hatching) into a second, final adult stage known as the spinner. This stage differentiates mayflies from all other species in the insect world. During this stage the adults swarm over the water, mate in the air, and culminate their life cycle. Spent, the males fall first onto the water, their outstretched wings getting trapped in the surface film. The females deposit their fertilized egg clusters into the water, and like the males, fall

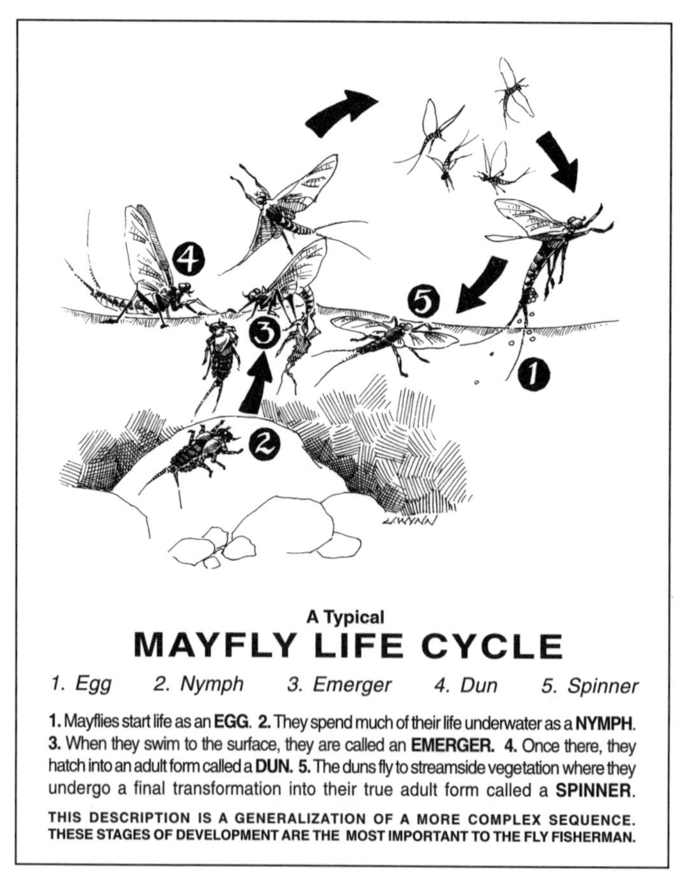

FIGURE 5.5

onto the water, too. At this point, their lives are over. Trout find the spinners an easily obtainable meal and need only to lie just under the surface of the water and sip in the now lifeless insects.

Spinner imitations should be characterized by outstretched wings so that the pattern's wing silhouette looks like an airplane. Spinner patterns are cast in a delicate presentation and fished with a drag-free drift.

Weather permitting, mayflies can be seen on the water from as early as February until as late as October. Once again, I cannot overemphasize the use of hatch charts to determine the appearance, size, color, and appropriate imitations of these insects.

As with caddisflies, a comprehensive hatch chart will prove indispensable to timing and identifying mayfly hatches. Mayfly hatches are dictated by the time of year and weather conditions. Their sizes and colors vary dramatically, so a well illustrated color identification book can be helpful, too. On a quality trout stream there can be as many as six or more different major hatches during the season. When you multiply the number of hatches by the stages of development, you have many combinations for the same mayfly. With this in mind, you can better appreciate the value of identification books and hatch charts. Using them will add to your angling pleasure by helping you identify, choose, and use the right patterns. Amateur entomology in itself can be a fun hobby.

SPECIALTY ITEMS AND FORAGE FISH

Crustaceans, which include crayfish, scuds, and sowbugs, damselflies, and dragonflies are among the categories that I refer to as specialty items. Although these food items should not be ignored, they do not usually play a major role in the rudiments of stream entomology. All of the aforementioned will entice trout from time to time, but do not plan your entire strategy around these minor players.

Frogs, mice, small snakes, and salamanders obviously constitute a huge meal for trout, and it is amazing to see even a small trout try to swallow one whole. Imitations can be fished on top like a dry fly or below the surface like a streamer. Be prepared for slashing strikes! Minnows, dace, shiners, and sculpins fall into the category of forage fish. They are best imitated by an artificial streamer, woolly bugger, or bucktail pattern. Primarily and most productively fished at first and last light, these offerings will be voraciously attacked by trout!

Matuka

One of the many questions that beginners ask is, what do you recommend as a general group of flies? Flyfishing instructor and owner of Henry's Fork Anglers in Idaho, Mike Lawson, told me, "It's been my experience that beginners tend to be intimidated by the volume of flies to choose from. They always want to know how to get started with a basic selection." As you can imagine, fly fishing situations vary dramatically across America; unfortunately, there is no one perfect answer. The question is further complicated by the extensive variety of patterns for the same fly, hook sizes, and color options. However, I feel the following "sweet sixteen" listed in (Figure 5.6) is as comprehensive a selection as you will need to get started.

I have suggested a variety of flies in this list; although you should

FIGURE 5.6

not purchase all 16 patterns in the same size and color. It is important for every angler, but especially for a beginner, to have a fly-buying plan. An up-to-date hatch chart and a phone call to the tackle shop that monitors the stream you are going to visit should provide you with the necessary information on the hook sizes and colors that will work best.

FLY TYING ADVICE

Artificial flies come in two general categories; dry flies that are made to float and wet flies that are made to sink. Fishing flies are constructed from bits of yarn, deer hair, tinsel, feathers or fur and are tied onto a hook with thread. They are fashioned to imitate the insects on which trout may feed.

Fly tying, like fly casting, is difficult to learn from a video tape, CD-ROM, or a book. It, too, requires basic hands-on instruction, and there are increasingly more classes available for beginners and experienced anglers alike. These courses are customarily held during the winter at local high schools and community colleges. The Federation of Fly Fishers and Trout Unlimited also offer lessons that are open to the public at reasonable fees.

Good Internet sources for fly tying are: Basic Fly Tying at http://www.mindspring.com~smarc; Gordon's Entomology Home Page at http://info.ex.ac.uk/~gj/ramel; Tom Juracek House of Fly Tying at http://www.ecentral.com/members/juracek; Mayfly Central at http://www.entm.purdue.edu/entomology/mayfly/mayfly.hind; Midwest Flytyer at http://www.mwflytyer.com; Roy's fly-fishing at http.//www. planet. eon.net/~ flyfish and www.Fly Tyer at http://kiene.com/flytyer. Other references can be found in, *200 Best Fly-Fishing Web Sites,* written by John A. Merry. This comprehensive work includes unbiased reviews of fly-fishing's finest internet offerings.

I recommend the instructional classes conducted by your neighborhood fly tackle dealer. Your local shop owner is a professional, and the classes he or she offers will be substantially more comprehensive and will include a fly tying manual. Most shops provide everything necessary to tie the fly patterns that will be taught during an evening's class. Should you want to buy your own fly tying equipment, all of the accessories and materials are immediately available for purchase at the shop. However, do not run out and make a huge investment in supplies until you are absolutely sure that you want to pursue this aspect of the sport.

Suppose you do want to tie your own flies. Stop and think about it. You are at home stuck on a tying problem or have some question in regard to a fly pattern. Your local dealer is only a phone call away and will be more than happy to answer your questions. No book or catalog can offer that kind of prompt, personal service.

As I discussed in the preface, almost every fly shop has a library of fly tying books and tapes. Many of these, however, are geared toward the advanced tier and often focus on one style only. If you have not learned the basics, which many of these books or tapes assume you have mastered, it is easy to get frustrated and be tempted to quit. Do yourself a favor. If you have any interest in tying at all, go to a local fly shop for instruction. Why not take your son, daughter, or a friend with you to share the experience?

A quick glance at the hatch chart for your favorite stream will indicate the specific flies and hook sizes that you may want to concentrate

WHAT'S IN A NAME?

Common names, their Latin-name equivalent and hook sizes.

Common Name	Size	Latin Name
Alderfly	12-14	Sialis spp.
Aquatic Worm	10-12	Oligochaeta
Black Quill	14	Leptophlebia cupida
Blue Quill	16	Paraleptophlebia adoptiva
Bluewinged Olive Dun	14	Drunella cornuta
Brown Drake	8-16	Ephemera simulans
Chocolate Dun	20	Serratella deficiens
Crane Fly • Midges Etc.	20	Diptera
Damselfly•Dragonfly	8-10	Odonata
Dark Green Drake	8-10	Litobrancha recurvata
Dobsonfly	6-10	Corydalus cornutus
Early Brown Stonefly	16	Strophopteryx fasciata
Fishfly	8-10	Megaloptera
Giant Black Stonefly	6-8	Pteronarcys dorsata
Golden Drake	12	Anthopotamus distinctus
Golden Stonefly	8-10	Calineuria californica
Grannom	12-14	Brachycentrus spp.
Gray Drake	12	Siphlonurus quebecensis
Great Stonefly	8-10	Agnetina capitata
Green Drake	6-10	Ephemera guttulata
Hendrickson/Red Quill	12-14	Ephemerella subvaria
Hex	6-8	Hexagenia limbata
Light Cahill	12-14	Stenacron interpunctatum
Little Black Caddisfly	18	Chimarra atterrima
Little Bluewinged Olive Dun	18-20	Baetis spp.
Little Yellow Stonefly	16	Isoperla spp.
March Brown	10-12	Stenonema vicarium
Micro Caddisflies	18-20	Hydroptilidae
Pale Evening Dun	14-16	Ephemerella invaria/E. rotunda
Pale Morning Dun	14-16	Ephemerella inermis/infrequens/lacustris
Pink Lady	12-14	Epeorus vitreus
Quill Gordon	12-14	Epeorus pleuralis
Salmonfly	6-8	Pteronarcys californica
Slate Drake	12	Isonychia bicolor
Slatewinged Olive	14	Drunella flavilinea
Specklewinged Dun	14-16	Callibaetis spp.
Sulphur	18	Ephemerella dorothea
Terrestrials	6-18	Coleoptera•Hymenoptera•Orthoptera
Trico	20-24	Tricorythodes spp.
White Fly	12-14	Ephoron leukon
Yellow Drake	10	Ephemera varia

FIGURE 5.7

on learning to tie first. You will also be pleasantly surprised to discover that you can learn to tie them in a six-week, twelve-hour course. You'll find a wide variety of materials, fly tying kits, and accessories priced to fit every budget and skill level. Let me emphasize that it doesn't take the most beautifully dressed fly to fool fish, so don't be discouraged if your initial efforts are not perfect. Believe me when I tell you that few things are more rewarding than catching a trout on a fly that you have tied.

Another area of entomology that invariably confuses fly fishermen is the use of an insect's common name which is usually different from the scientific name of a particular insect species. Unfortunately, there is no universal language in our sport. For example, one fisherman may use an insect's Latin name where another angler will refer to the fly by its common name. The same fly may even have a regional or a colloquial name. Therefore, this reference list (Figure 5.7) may be helpful to you.

Special thanks go to Professor Greg Hoover for his many contributions to this chapter including the work on this list.

Greg is a Pennsylvania State University entomologist who lives in Lemont, Pennsylvania near State College. He did his undergraduate work at Mansfield State and pursued graduate studies at Penn State. Greg has authored numerous scientific papers, published articles in *American Angler* magazine, co-authored the book *Great Rivers Great Hatches*, contributed two chapters to the book *Limestone Legends* and is currently working on a new project that deals with mayfly distribution in Pennsylvania. Greg is a veteran angler with over thirty years of on-stream experience. He is a master at reading a stream, recognizing prime trout habitat and identifying insects and Greg is a superb fly tier too. His study flies are simply beautiful. He is the faculty adviser to the Penn State Fly Fishing Club and truly enjoys working with young people. Greg loves to teach and is always willing to share his knowledge with others. He is a regular guest speaker with such groups as the Theodore Gordon Fly Fishers, Trout Unlimited and the Mainline Fly Tyers. Above all, Greg Hoover is a professional and a gentleman in every sense of the word. If you ever have the chance to attend one of his seminars, don't miss the opportunity–you won't be disappointed!

Will The Real "Mr. Ants" Please Stand Up!

Necessity, who is the mother of invention.

– Plato

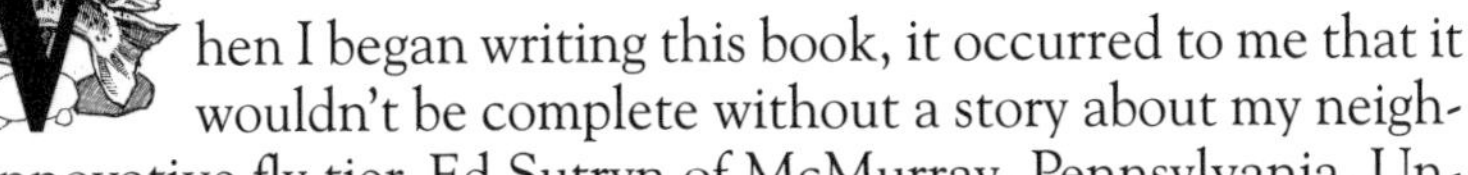

When I began writing this book, it occurred to me that it wouldn't be complete without a story about my neighbor, the innovative fly tier, Ed Sutryn of McMurray, Pennsylvania. Unfortunately, when I finally got around to finding him, I discovered he had moved out of town.

Upset with myself for procrastinating and losing the opportunity to meet him, I decided to drive up to the local fly shop to see if anyone there knew where he was living. On the way I couldn't help thinking about the contribution that Ed has made to our sport.

Back in the mid 1950s Ed and his brother-in-law, Stan Walters, were angling at Fishing Creek near Lamar, Pennsylvania. While working a slow stretch of water under a sprawling oak Ed brushed a few ants off his vest. Within casting distance, a dozen brook trout were taking something from the surface. Ed remarked, "There were so many rise forms that it looked like it was raining." Hours later and still fishless, Ed was as disgusted as he'd been in quite a while, so he and Stan quit fishing for the day. The long drive home seemed to take forever. The conversation centered around their inability to catch a fish. That night it dawned on Ed that those brookies were sipping ants that were falling from the tree above him. "The only ant patterns available back then were made from silk thread or fur. Unfortunately, they were nearly impossible to see on the water and sank too quickly. I knew I could design something better," Ed thought. The next morning Ed went straight to his tying desk. Using two small pieces of cork, he hand fashioned body segments, painted them black, then, carefully threading and gluing them onto a short piece of nylon, he tied them on to a hook, adding a few turns of chicken hackle to resemble legs. The pattern looked great and worked even better. Four years later, Ed reluctantly switched to balsa wood for the bodies. He remembered, "cork became scarce and the price got too high." Ed christened his new creation the "McMurray Ant" in honor of the town where he resided. To this day, Ed's ant continues to be one of the most productive patterns ever invented. As a matter of fact, his ant pattern proved to be so successful and unique it was granted United States Patent number 3323248.

Still sulking over my lost opportunity, I pulled into the parking lot at the shop. Right there in front of my eyes sat an old Chevy pickup with a license plate that read "Mr. Ants." It was my lucky day! I jumped out of my truck, ran up the stairs and nearly flew through the door. I saw Rich Roseborough, the owner, speaking to a tall, lanky, silver-haired man who was the only other person in the place. I knew from magazine photographs that he wasn't Ed, so you can just imagine my surprise when

John Steinhart

Rich introduced me to John "Mr. Ants" Steinhart.

"Steiney," as he is affectionately nicknamed, is a private man who is gentle, quiet and shy. He and Lucille, his wife of 40 plus years, reside in Carnegie, Pennsylvania where they raised their four children. John worked in the cable and installation department of the old Bell Telephone Company for 38 years, but in 1985 he opted to take an early retirement. Since then he's been fishing full-time and loving every minute of it. At the age of sixty-eight Steiney is fit as a fiddle and has ample energy to put in the 100 odd days a year that he logs on the trout streams.

Having fished for decades, John grew up with the sport during the infancy of mass-produced flies. The commercial flies that were available in fly fishing shops were often expensive and of poor quality. "Back then we were using balsa and cork bodies for terrestrials, but they fell apart too soon," Steiney told me. In the case of the McMurray Ant, for example, Steiney remembered, "If you lost one ball, the fly floated funny, and the fish wouldn't take it."

In 1975, Steiney began to experiment with different materials to develop a fly that would last, yet was effective and easy to tie. Shortly thereafter he started to use foam, and his first attempt was a caddisfly that worked surprisingly well. As time went on, John discovered a way

Ed Sutryn

to solidly attach the foam onto the hook, fashion the proportionally-segmented bodies and heads, and use chicken hackle and turkey feathers (biots) to refine his creations. After much trial and error, he finally developed a set of terrestrials that seem to last forever and are productive, too. The unique feature of his flies is the realistic underbody that seems to drive the trout crazy. His trade name, "Instant Ants," progressed to "Instant Crickets," and over the years, his collection has expanded to include beetles and caterpillars. Steiney considers the latter to be the most productive. Years ago, John gave so many of them away that the word quickly spread among the angling fraternity. As a result, he soon had dealers all over the country wanting to order some for their shops.

John Steinhart will never receive the same recognition that his fly tying contemporaries have, but that's exactly the way he wants it. He isn't in it for the money. "It's just a hobby that got out of hand," Steiney told me. At least one of his terrestrial patterns appeared recently in an article in a national publication. Unfortunately, he was not credited for the original pattern, but the oversight didn't seem to bother him. "I really don't care nor want to tie flies for sale anymore," Steinhart confided. I for one, though, sure hope he passes on his knowledge before he hangs up his bobbin.

Talking to Steiney rekindled my interest in finding Ed Sutryn, and I finally caught up with Ed at his new home in Wyomissing, Pennsylvania.

Born in 1916, Edmund Michael Sutryn was raised in the Pennsylvania coal mining town of Shamokin, near Reading. Ed told me he had a typical upbringing for a kid growing up in a small town.

"I didn't have time to get into trouble because I practiced and played the clarinet in the Coal Township High School Band," Ed reminisced. His father's boss didn't own a car, so it became Ed's job to chauffeur him to all of the local trout streams. There Ed got a chance to try his hand at casting and received his introduction to fly fishing. Ed's enthusiasm and love for the sport grew.

"The day before the Japanese attacked Pearl Harbor, I was knee deep in the north branch of the Susquehanna River catching fish. The day after, I was drafted into the United States Army," Ed told me. "My clarinet playing paid off. The company commander took a liking to me and asked if I wanted to join his band. Believe it or not, making music kept me out of basic training."

Ed fished every stream near the camps where he was stationed, and when the order finally came for him to go overseas, he immediately phoned home and asked his mother to buy that $4, six piece, "no name," fly rod at the local auto supply store and send it and his reel to him.

"I was probably the only G.I. that took fishing tackle to Europe during the war," Ed told me. He had the opportunity to fly fish in Austria, Bavaria and France. In Italy, he started to run out of tying material. With no fly shops around, he put his Yankee ingenuity to work. "I taught myself enough Italian to converse with a local farmer," Ed recalled, "and I asked him if I could purchase some feathers from one of his chickens. '*Tu sei pazzo,*' the farmer said. He thought I was crazy, until I showed him a fly and explained what I wanted to do. The farmer had his son catch a rooster, and I plucked all of the hackle that I needed. You have to make the best of every situation," Ed said proudly! "Most of the fishing I did was after the war ended when I was stationed in

Schwabmunchen, Bavaria. One of the best trout streams I ever fished flowed through town and I fished all day, everyday, for the next two or three months."

When Ed got back to the states, he returned to Shamokin. Within a few years he moved to Pittsburgh and then to McMurray, a rural farming town approximately 15 miles south of Pittsburgh. He started working for the Railway Mail Service in 1949, and six years later he married Hope Walters. They had two children, Dan and Gary. In the 20-odd years that followed, Ed kept making flies in between his Pittsburgh and New York mail runs and on his days off. "It was hard to keep up with all the orders," Ed remembered. "I had people from all over calling me for flies." Letters and requests poured in from across the United States. Some came from as far away as Australia, England, France, and Japan.

Ed retired from the Railway Mail Service in 1976. In 1987 the Sutryns decided to move to Wyomissing, Pennsylvania to be closer to their sons and the many trout streams that Ed loves to fish.

This quiet and unpretentious eighty-three-year-old is in great shape and still makes all of the bodies for his world famous flies by hand. Like many of the fly fishing and fly tying pioneers of his generation, Ed is totally unimpressed by his accomplishments. *Fly Fisherman Magazines* Contributing Editor Art Lee wrote, "To my way of thinking, if Sutryn never came up with another idea, his McMurray Ant would be enough to establish him as one of fly-rodding's true innovators." Modestly, Ed told me, "I've enjoyed tying flies all my life although I never took a lesson." Ed likes angling at Tulpehocken Creek and the Little Lehigh and says simply that "fly fishing is a great way to relax." I for one wish him many more years of good health and good fishing.

Chapter Six

Where The Trout Live

This is what fishing is all about. It is in developing and refining knowledge of the fish themselves and, with this understanding, finding ways of taking them that shows them at their best.

– Roderick Haig-Brown

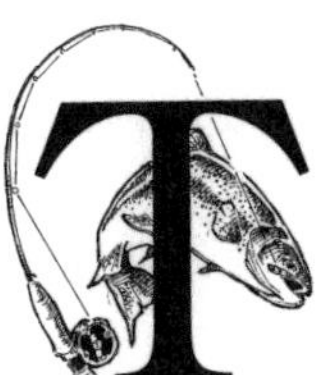

The specific areas in a trout stream where fish can be found are called lies. By and large, trout will be in similar positions in moving water no matter where you fish. When you can recognize the fundamental places where trout should be, you will eliminate approximately 90 percent of the unproductive water. This knowledge will enable you to spend your valuable time on stream catching fish rather than looking for them.

Nationally acclaimed author, fly fishing authority and *Fly Rod & Reel Magazine's* 1995 Angler of the Year Gary LaFontaine gives us sage advice when he says, "If any fly fisherman, beginner to advanced, would take five or even ten minutes sitting next to the stream and just watching the water before beginning to cast, he or she would fish better the whole day. The big mistake is that so few do."

Award-winning author and casting instructor Robert Nastasi agrees and adds, "Beginners need to understand the trout, its habits and habitat. The most common error a beginner makes approaching a river or stream is to immediately start fishing. I would never let a student 'string-up' at the car. I would always make them wait until they reached the stream bank and took a look at what was happening."

It is always to your benefit to observe the water to see if trout are actively taking flies on the surface, referred to as "rising" or "working on top." If they are not, you can be sure that the fish are feeding underneath the surface because trout feed day and night. If fish are working on top, you should use a dry fly pattern that imitates the natural insects that they are feeding on. The use of an insect net (seine) while on stream, or a monocular or binoculars, will help you see and possibly identify the insects better at a safe distance without frightening the fish.

If there is no surface activity, yet you still want to fish on top, you may choose to fish the water by casting your fly to likely spots in the hope of soliciting the attention of an unseen trout. For this approach, select a dry fly attractor pattern such as a Royal Wulff, Humpy, Stimulator or an Irresistible. Another alternative would be to fish the water with a soft hackle, nymph or streamer under the surface. A productive way to cover the water thoroughly is by fishing the clock (Figure 6.1). This technique, as described by Doug Swisher, is a variation of fishing the water and can be achieved by casting to the seven positions pictured in this illustration. If you don't get a strike after five or so attempts at each spot, simply move five yards upstream and start the process again. One of the unique aspects of this approach is that you can use any fly in your box, although the best results should be attained by using the patterns indicated on the hatch chart for the time of year and stream you are fishing. Once you learn to recognize where the trout are most likely to be, your fly selection and fishing technique will be determined by whether you choose to fish on top or beneath the surface.

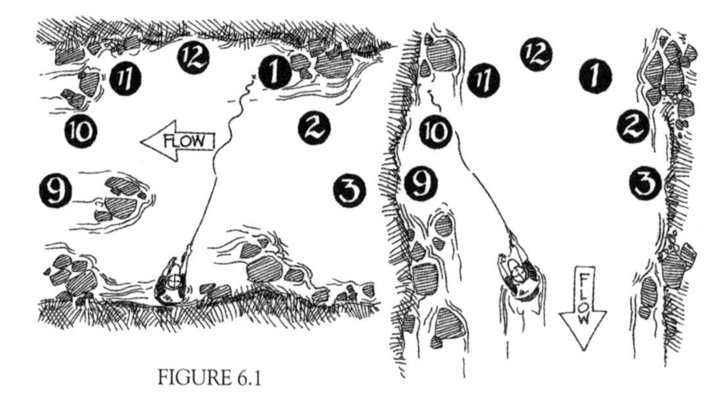

FIGURE 6.1

Joan Wulff and George Anderson, owner of the Yellowstone Angler, agree that beginners spend far too much time fishing in one place. Their suggestion is to cover the water and keep moving.

Experience will teach you that fish cannot swim endlessly where the current flows strongest. Often this position is in the middle of the stream. It can be located by casting your fly line straight across to the opposite bank. You will quickly see a big curve form in your fly line where the water is flowing most swiftly. This same spot can also be determined by observing the bubble line or any floating debris. Trout are creatures of habit and are very territorial, especially when feeding. Therefore, you will notice that they often congregate in the shallow water near the bank. Keep in mind that trout are continuously alert for predators that could come at them from the bank or swoop down on them from the sky. This innate fear causes them to seek cover that affords protection and ideally provides them with a constant supply of food.

The 12 fundamental places in a trout stream most likely to hold fish are called feeding, holding, sheltering or prime lies. I call them the "Delightful Dozen" (Figure 6.2). These locations provide some combination of or, in the case of a prime lie, all the basics of shelter from danger: a relatively constant food supply, well-oxygenated water of optimal temperature and reasonable comfort away from fast current.

1. **Feeder mouth.** One overlooked area where fish tend to gather is at the confluence of flows. This is especially true if the water that's coming in is colder than the main stream as inlets typically are. This lie potentially doubles the amount of food and highly oxygenated water available to the fish that usually lie facing upstream near the mouth.

2. **Pools.** Deep pools offer the trout optimum protection from predators. As the water gets warmer and more shallow elsewhere, the deeper pools usually remain cooler, and fish tend to move there for cover. Pools are divided into three sections: the head, a prime lie; the belly, a sheltering lie; and the tail, a feeding lie. Each of these areas can hold fish.

3. **Dams.** You can find trout lying directly in front of and below and downstream of the spillway of a dam. The bank-to-bank expanse immediately ahead of a dam is a perfect holding spot because of the slow moving water. In high water, or a lengthy and steep vertical drop, the tumult below a dam often creates a plunge pool and churns up the stream bottom, dislodging food organisms that make an easily obtainable meal for the trout. The area under the turbulence or just downstream of this section, like the belly of a pool, is where you will most likely find some of the biggest fish in the stream.

4. **Pocket water.** Trout can also be found in the quiet zone directly in front of or in the pocket behind a surface protruding obstruction where the water movement is virtually at a standstill. Obstructions slow down the current and channel food back to the waiting fish.

5. **Weed beds and emergent vegetation.** Weed beds anywhere in a stream provide excellent cover and a continuous supply of crustaceans, including crayfish, scuds, sowbugs, and many species of swimming mayfly nymphs. Emergent vegetation like cattails offer shade from the sun, protection from predators and habitat for aquatic and terrestrial insects.

FIGURE 6.2

This drawing depicts several hundred feet of trout stream.
It could contain any or all of the lies described in the illustration.

6. Deflectors. A man-made or man-placed deflector, such as a rectangular concrete block, telephone pole, log or boulder slows the speed of the water and channels food organisms to trout lying within its proximity.

7. Runs. A run is the transitional section of increasingly deeper moving water found just beyond a riffle (see Number 12) and ahead of a pool. It often flows over large submerged rocks which provide good cover and slow the velocity of the underwater current. This section is usually food rich and is an important holding and feeding area for fish.

8. Flats. Trout sometimes prefer the slow-moving slack water of a flat because the movement is slight and they need to expend little energy to hold their position. You will recognize this stretch because the top water is typically as smooth as glass. However, fish are extremely wary in this calm water as they hold stationary or cruise around looking for food.

9. Obstructions. Another great place to find trout would be in front of, behind or to the side of any natural obstacles in the water. These obstructions can be fallen trees or submerged rocks. Like all deflectors, they, too, slow down the current and channel food to the fish.

10. Edges and bends. As we learned earlier in this chapter, trout often congregate close to the edges in feeding lies. Frequently, outside banks are undercut, specifically those around a sharp bend. This area is an ideal place for big fish to lie. It offers the fish optimal protection from predators and is an excellent hideaway from which they can ambush food that may drift or swim by. Never forget that trout are predators.

11. Riparian vegetation. Fish can often be found under overhanging tree limbs or streamside vegetation, especially near banks. These spots offer shade from the sun, protection from predators and are often a great place to intercept food that accidentally falls into the water.

12. Riffles. There are usually rocky, shallow stretches of water in most trout streams. As the water cascades over the small stones, the surface becomes very choppy and shimmers as the light reflects off each small wave. This portion of the stream is known as a riffle, and trout tend to congregate at the tail end. Fish feel safe in the riffles because the rocks slow the current, and as the water tumbles over the irregular shapes, the broken surface provides cover for the fish, making them less visible to both predators and fishermen. This location is the most likely place to find hatching insects because riffles are the principal food producing hot spots in streams. Shallow water promotes photosynthesis while the rocks help generate life-sustaining oxygen. Both are critical to emerging insect life and the trout that feed on them.

There are a number of secondary places where fish can be found. Several important examples follow:

1. Rip-rap. A rip-rap is a man-made deflector that is designed to fill in and hold back eroding stream banks. It is constructed primarily of logs or stone chunks held together by wire mesh baskets shaped into large rectangular blocks (Gabions). You may find trout lying anywhere along its length.

2. Eddy. An eddy is a swirl of water usually found near the bank. Eddies are created by deflected water turning back against the flow. This whirlpool action churns up a great number of food organisms that make for an easily obtainable meal. Drifting insects present an easy target for opportunistic fish. Be aware that the reverse currents can make for challenging fishing.

3. Slick. A slick is the faster running, but glassy smooth, water found near the tail end of a pool. Fish often rest and feed here.

4. Tongue. A tongue is a V-shaped narrow length of flat, swiftly-moving water that is often found flowing between two obstructions.

5. Channel. A channel is a deep, usually narrow, faster-moving flow of water found between islands, banks and large boulders.

After looking at the condensed "Delightful Dozen" illustration, and trying to digest all of this information, a few students have still asked, if trout can be found in all these places, where don't they live? Without exception, trout can't survive in stagnant or polluted or warm water. Although there are exceptions, trout don't frequent long stretches of water exposed to direct sunlight. You will rarely find trout lying along a smooth stream bottom without cover or inside submerged weed beds. Trout avoid low banks and those chocked with silt. In addition, trout don't lie along edges that are devoid of grasses or sedges or riparian vegetation. A swift, shallow and turbulent run with a steep gradient is poor trout habitat and you won't find trout in riffles or sandbars that aren't deep enough to allow the fish to swim. Last, trout can't live in streams without a healthy insect population or some constant food supply.

I recommend the following books to every angler, but especially to anyone interested in further study on this subject. *Fishing Dry Flies for Trout on Rivers and Streams* by Art Lee, and *Reading Trout Streams* by Tom Rosenbauer.

How To See Trout In The Water

Being able to see and cast to trout, referred to as "sight fishing," increases your chances of catching one. Now that you know where trout are usually found, how can you best observe them under the surface? Anglers must position themselves in such a way as to minimize glare without casting a shadow when they look into the water. To help eliminate glare, Lefty Kreh suggests, "You should tilt your head slightly to one side or the other as you look into the water." Trout can camouflage themselves with an almost supernatural ability, and spotting them is a skill that takes time to develop.

As we discussed in chapter two, polarized sunglasses with side shields, a wide brimmed hat with a dark, non-reflective underbrim and clothing that blends in with your surroundings, coupled with a cautious approach, are vital ingredients to stalking the stream and locating trout. However, the fish's movement is the key to finding them. The motion could be as obvious as the flash from a rolling trout or as subtle as a fanning tail. Fish seldom reveal themselves entirely; therefore, you must train your eyes to look for hints of their presence–any unusual shapes or lines that look out of place. For example, the darkened outline of a head, tail, the edge of a fin or even a shadow on the stream bottom could indicate a trout. If you notice anything that appears "fishy," concentrate your attention on that area for a few minutes before moving on.

THE pH FACTOR AND WATER TEMPERATURE

The pH factor, the designation of the hydrogen ion concentration in the water, is part of the chemical balance of water and has much to do with the viability of insect and fish life in a trout stream. A range of pH values between six and eight is desirable. Fish mortality may occur at a pH factor below five because the water is too acidic. A reading above eight may be too alkaline and will eventually kill fish, too. Spring creeks are usually alkaline whereas freestone streams are by and large acidic. The better waters tend to be those that are more alkaline.

The last piece of information that the intelligent angler needs to know is the trout's favorite temperature range. Locating that optimal temperature, and where it coincides with the trout's basic needs will determine where you will most likely find fish. According to the dean of American fly fishing, the late Lee Wulff, "Harry Darbee wet-waded the Beaverkill River which allowed him to feel the temperature differences." In effect, Mr. Darbee became a "human thermometer," able to find the cooler temperatures that trout prefer. The ideal water temperature for brook, brown and rainbow trout ranges between 55 to 65 degrees Fahrenheit. Fish are cold-blooded, so temperatures below 50 degrees Fahrenheit slow their metabolism and digestion to the point that they often become lethargic and unable to swim well. However, there are a few notable exceptions. Gary Borger points out that, "The San Juan River, for example, never gets above 45 degrees Fahrenheit and the fish there are really big and fight very well." Sustained temperatures of above 70 degrees Fahrenheit normally drive trout into deep pools, cooler feeder mouths and spring inlets, or the shaded areas upstream toward the colder headwaters. Therefore, unless you are certain of a stream's suitability,[15] you will find using a thermometer to be very helpful in determining where to begin fishing.

15. For example, state stocked streams must meet certain biological criteria and can be assumed to be at least seasonable "safe" places to fish.

W.WYNN

EARL "DUKE" SHAPIRO

We forget that our sport has its roots in medieval chivalry, that its best artifacts are the work of artisans rather than technology.

– Ernest Schwiebert

It is almost impossible to believe that the hands that restore priceless antique cars are the same ones that also build classic fly fishing reels. Who could possess such skill?

Earl Shapiro is an extremely private man who lives with his wife and daughter in a Pittsburgh suburb. Every day for the past 35 years Earl has walked to his garage where he performs auto body magic on priceless vehicles like Lagondas, Duesenbergs and Rolls Royces. There is no doubt that he loves vintage automobiles, but equally important to Earl is his passion for fine fly rods and reels. Fly fishing since the early '60s, "Duke," as he is affectionately nicknamed, purchased his first bamboo rod in 1971 from a Mills catalog. The action, appearance and enjoyment of that first rod were so captivating to him that in 1981 Earl became a Leonard Rod Company representative.

To complement the cane rods he was fishing with, Earl started using old fly fishing reels. For years his labor of love has been repairing and restoring these classic beauties for his own and a few friends' use. Earl feels that master reelmakers like Meek, Vom Hofe and Walker had a love for and a pride in craftsmanship that, with the exception of Stanley Bogdan and a few others, is rarely seen today.

Sure, many of today's reels are exceptional, but as Earl mentioned, "Old reels, like old cars, live, breathe, have personality and soul. Each has a unique story to tell if you only take the time to listen." They also share something else in common, each one needs care and attention. Earl explained that "every old reel I have seen had something wrong with it. They were used, neglected and often abused, but I love to fix them." Repairs range from a simple tuneup to a complete overhaul. "It could be a full-time job for me," he remarked. Unfortunately, people don't appreciate the expertise required and hours involved in repairing them. Consequently, no one wants to pay for the time it takes to do the repairs.

"When I accept a reel repair, I want it to be perfect," Earl said. "I'm responsible for it and want to do it right, so it lasts forever for its owner." Unfortunately, there just isn't enough time to restore cars and repair reels, too, complained Earl. One day a few years ago Earl said to me, "Before I die, I want to make a reel." Quite frankly, I forgot all about his comment, but months later he called and said, "Come over, I've got something to show you." I fully expected to see some interesting new car restoration, but instead I was presented with a small leather bag. I opened it. At first glance, I thought his wife and daughter who deal in collectible jewelry had found a little treasure in an old cigar box along with Roosevelt campaign buttons, fancy old fountain pens and cracked, yellowed pictures of people long deceased. Instead, it was a reel, and it looked exactly like a Meek No. 44, only it was shiny, sparkling, and brand new. It was exquisite! I grinned in disbelief, but Earl finally convinced me that this was the reel that he had challenged himself to make. Earl explained, "When I made that reel and those that followed, I did it for myself and not for anyone else. I just wanted to see if I had the perseverance and ability to do it. I truly don't care if another person in the world sees them. As a matter of fact, I wish I could have kept them a secret from everybody, I guess I'm different that way. Unfortunately for me, I had to try them out to see if they worked. Others saw them and now want to buy one. Please understand that I still only make them for my own enjoyment and personal use.

I'm sure there are a handful of people today who could duplicate what he's done, but where does one find nickel silver, ivory and Bakelite? This reel, along with others Earl has made since 1992, have been faithfully and painstakingly reproduced using original materials and with meticulous attention paid to every detail. Earl scours the classified section of the newspaper, and he knows every metal supplier on the East Coast. In addition, Earl goes to antique shops, auctions, house sales and has all his friends keeping an eye out for material.

The differences between classic reels and Duke's aren't visible, but they can be felt and heard. He has incorporated the best features of the old reels and added innovations of his own. For example, his adjustable drag system works with or without the click on, ensuring that the spool will not over-run causing the fly line to backlash. His gears have 24 teeth so the reel runs as smooth as silk and doesn't sound like an old coffee grinder. Talk about smooth and quiet: one of his latest creations is a ball bearing model. But his crowning achievement is a 2-inch trout multiplier with a centered handle that he made to use out West. He told me, "It was so tedious and time consuming I wish I could have quit and thrown it away. If you could see the inside of this reel, you'd understand. It was so difficult that I'll never make another one."

All this considered, Earl's reels are as aesthetically beautiful as their classic counterparts. However, they are mechanically superior and should last forever.

Years ago, countries, people and their products were as varied as their languages, customs and appearances. Unfortunately, today we live in a world of mass production that clamors for efficiency and uniformity. Computer technology, automation and duplication leave little room for originality and individual expression, so it is refreshing to see someone come along who has crafted something that is beautiful as well as functional and to know that his motivation is not self-serving. You see, Shapiro reels are not for sale.

J.WYNN

Chapter Seven

Reading The Water

An experienced trout fisherman can glance at a section of stream and predict where the most and best trout will be . . . This skill is called "reading the water" an especially appropriate phrase because, to the expert, a stream is an open book.

– Leonard M. Wright, Jr.

When college football announcer Ron Franklin appears on ESPN's "Outdoors" Saturday mornings, one segment from his spring television show "The Sportsman's Challenge" was titled "Intellifishing." Obviously the word is a neologism combining the words intelligent and fishing. I want to borrow it from him because it is applicable to this teaching section.

When a trout takes a fly on or just under the water's surface, water is displaced. As a result, a rise form is visible to the perceptive angler. Rise forms are the tell-tale disturbances, like rings or splashes, that help us find the fish and "read the water." They reveal a lot of information about the specific stage of an insect's development.

Top-water dry-fly fishing, in my opinion, is the most exciting aspect of this sport because it is so visually satisfying. There is something magical about the instant a trout rises and takes your fly. That moment is the culmination of your angling education and experience and will, I hope, be a thrilling and successful one for you, too. Fish feed day and night, and the technique that you use to catch them will vary to the extent that they are actively taking flies on or beneath the surface. Although most trout are caught under the surface using nymphs and streamers, quality trout streams will frequently have fish "working on top," their rise forms visible, or at least "looking up," lying close to the surface. I say looking up because, oftentimes, a fish can be induced to rise and strike by using a top-water attractor pattern.

RISE FORMS

The following six drawings and accompanying explanations, depict the basic rise forms that trout leave on top of the water. The first five sketches represent surface feeding, and the sixth portrays emerger feeding, barely under the surface. I have also included general sideview illustrations of what a rising trout could look like as it takes the fly. Last, I suggest the types of insects upon which the trout may be feeding.

Head and Tail

The head and tail rise form results when a trout, lying close to the surface, arcs up slowly and deliberately to take insects trapped in the film. The fishes neb (or nose), then its dorsal fin and back, followed by its tail (which waves slightly as the fish slips back under) can be seen as the trout swims in a porpoise-like motion (Figure 7.1a). This leisurely rise is primarily found in slower-moving water as the trout takes emerging midge pupae or nymphs, stillborns or mayfly spinners (Figure 7.1b).

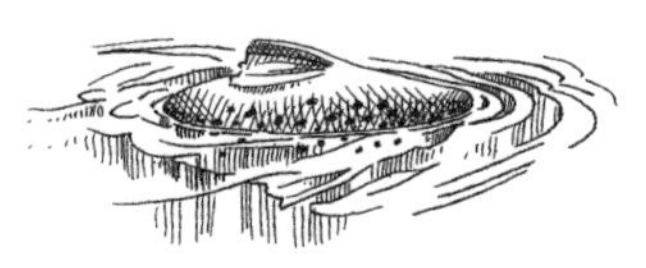

Surface Disturbance
FIGURE 7.1a

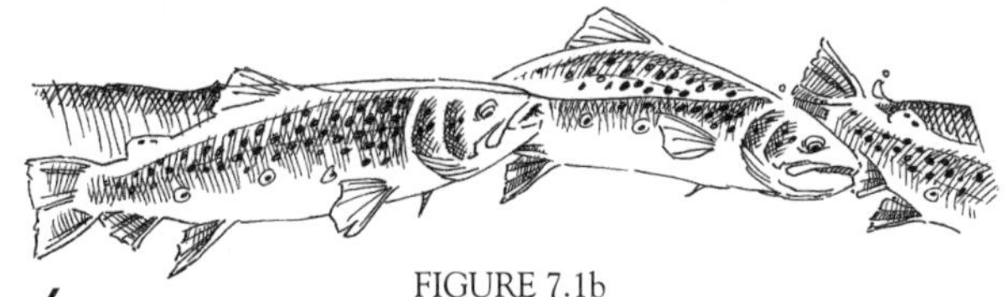

FIGURE 7.1b

Standard

The standard, or simple rise, is the most common rise form and looks like a rain drop has fallen on the water (Figure 7.2a). It is characterized by concentric circles or rings that ebb across the top of the water. This form is caused by the fish's neb breaking through the surface. It is the rise form that trout ordinarily leave after having taken an insect like a mayfly dun, emerger or a floating nymph from the surface (Figure 7.2b).

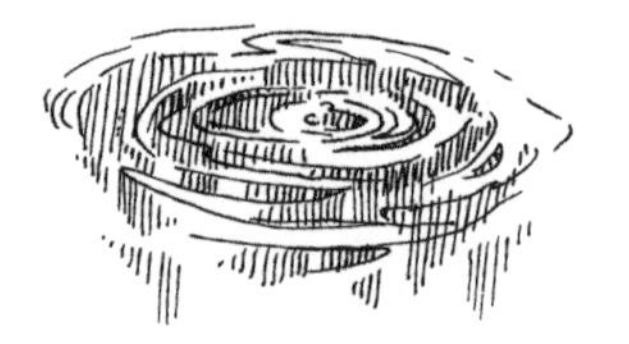

Surface Disturbance
FIGURE 7.2a

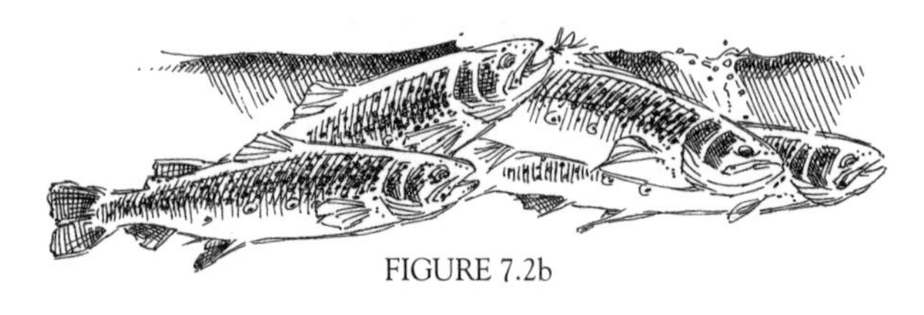

FIGURE 7.2b

Sip

The sip, or kiss, is the most difficult of all the rise forms to see because it is very subtle (Figure 7.3a). The water surface is barely penetrated by the fish's neb and only a few small rings, if any, may appear. Little water is displaced as a trout holding just below the surface leisurely tips up to take insects like midges, mayfly spinners, floating nymphs or emergers that are trapped in the film just beneath the surface. The opening and closing of the fish's mouth as it takes in both water and a small amount of air produces an audible noise similar to the sound of a soft kiss. On dark evenings an angler can often locate trout by listening for this sound. Because of the abundance of food and the trout's close proximity to the surface, the feeding lane will be very narrow so casting accuracy is imperative (Figure 7.3b).

Surface Disturbance
FIGURE 7.3a

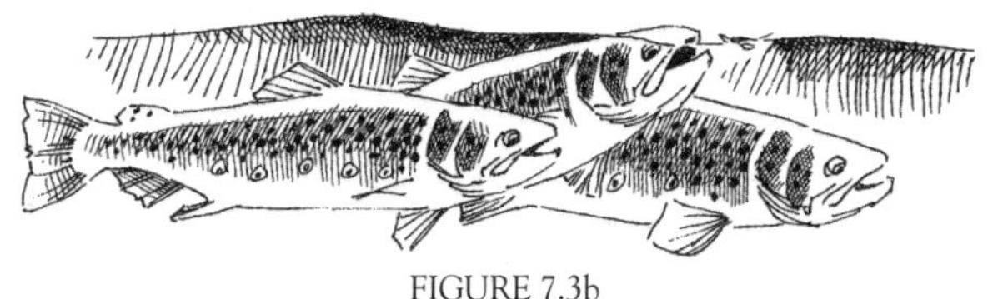

FIGURE 7.3b

Slash

The slash, also referred to as a splashy rise, is made by a trout as it torpedoes upward through the water to intercept an emerging nymph (Figure 7.4a). The fish's momentum often causes it to uncharacteristically come out of the water. A splash which can be easily seen and heard at a distance could also be the result of a trout slashing at a caddisfly or any large active insect as it flutters its wings before hurriedly lifting off the surface (Figure 7.4b).

Surface Disturbance
FIGURE 7.4a

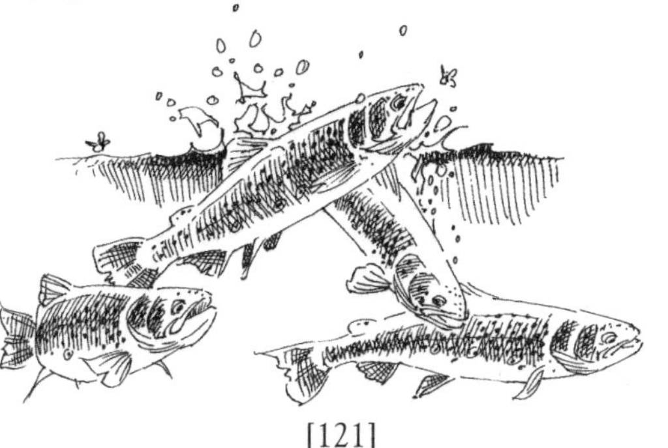

FIGURE 7.4b

Swirl

The swirl rise form is caused by a trout taking an insect, like a terrestrial, from just below or on the surface and turning quickly to return to its lie (Figure 7.5a). Caddisflies and floating stoneflies, such as the ones you would find on the McKenzie River in Oregon, can be taken in this manner, too (Figure 7.5b).

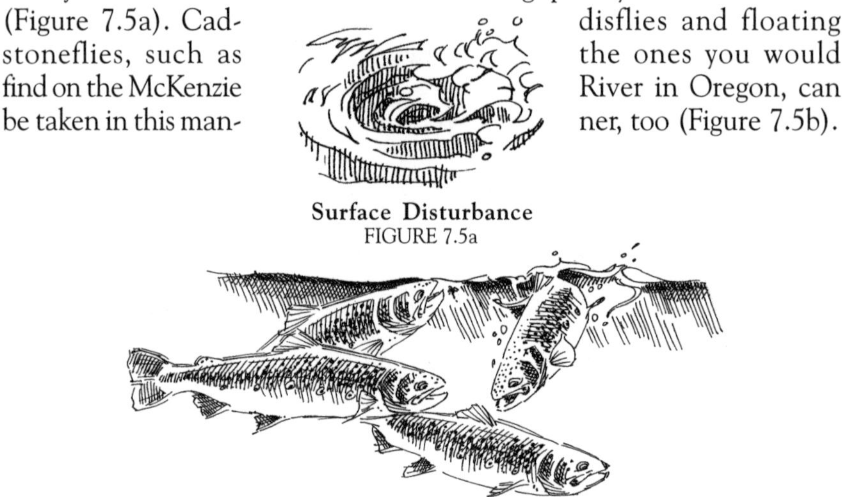

Surface Disturbance
FIGURE 7.5a

FIGURE 7.5b

Bulge

The bulge rise form occurs when a trout lying inches beneath the top of the water tips up slightly to take small insects from just under the surface (Figure 7.6a). The surface disturbance looks like a small swirl in the middle of what appears to be a hump of water, followed by a tiny whirlpool as insects like nymphs, small mayflies, micro caddisflies or midge pupae are taken into the trout's mouth (Figure 7.6b).

Surface Disturbance
FIGURE 7.6a

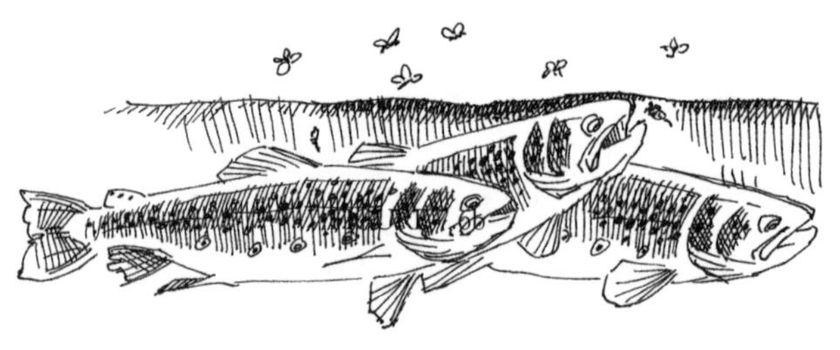

FIGURE 7.6b

There are other rise forms that you should be aware of, too. Just like the slash or splash, the boil results from a trout intercepting emerging insects, but without breaking through the surface. The rise form looks exactly like boiling water, small bubbles or a choppy surface in a concentrated area. In contrast, a trout foraging on the stream bottom or in a weed bed can alert you to its presence by its tail protruding through the surface.

Please keep in mind that there are very few absolutes in this sport. These illustrations, rise form explanations and suggested insects are good choices; however, a trout's behavior can and will vary. Remember, fish are as unpredictable a creature as God put on this Earth.

As you examine the water for rising trout, be on the lookout for airborne insects especially over the riffles. As we learned in chapter six, riffles are the principal food producing hot spots in a trout stream and newly emerging insects as well as the spinner stage of mayflies can be found there.

Clusters of bubbles are formed in the riffles, too. They appear white in color, and to the uninitiated, look like soap suds as they drift downstream. These clumps of foam, or for that matter any floating debris, follow precise channels or seams. The bubble line(s) designates food concentrations on or below the surface that flow into feeding lies to trout holding on either side. In addition, bubbles help us see the subtle changes of direction, like eddies, and can indicate the speed of the water and path of the current.

The following chart, "The Process of Elimination", is a checklist outlining a logical series of steps to follow when choosing alternate flies after your original selection has been rejected (Figure 7.7). Please note the importance that variations play in your decision to abandon a pat-

DRY FLY SELECTION

PROCESS OF ELIMINATION

If five drag free drifts prove unsuccessful, try imparting a brief, subtle movement to the fly on two additional casts. The trout's reaction, or lack thereof, should influence your decision making process, too.

BEFORE YOU ABANDON YOUR INITIAL SELECTION TRY THESE FOUR STEPS:

1. SIZE

Change to a smaller imitation of the identical pattern.
For example: change from a size 14 to a size 16.

2. SHAPE

Change to another style of the same pattern.
For example: change from a comparadun to a parachute.

3. TIPPET

Change to a smaller diameter or lengthen it.
For example: change from a 5X to 6X or increase length.

4. COLOR

Change to a darker or lighter shade of the identical pattern.
For example: change from yellow to green or vice versa.

IF ALL THIS FAILS, CHANGE PATTERNS.

FIGURE 7.7

tern. Remember, small differences often trigger positive responses from the fish.

What should you do when trout continue to rise and you have exhausted the "process?" Change patterns or quit fishing? It is easy for anyone to become exasperated, especially someone just starting out. Therefore, I have a few suggestions to try before you give up. First, something as simple as changing the angle of your casting presentation may bring results. Try moving your position in the stream slightly and see if the new approach works. Second, during a heavy hatch or spinner fall, your fly may get lost in the crowd. Dig down into your fly box and find an attractor pattern that is in stark contrast to the flies that are hatching. Trout are predators and the new look may cause a strike. Last, don't forget to grease your fly and leader (but never the tippet) with lots of floatant and twitch or skitter the fly near the fish. This can be achieved by making short tugs on the fly line or shaking the rod briefly to impart movement to the fly. This imitation of a struggling insect may attract the attention of an opportunistic trout. If these suggestions don't work, move to another section of the stream.

KNOW YOUR QUARRY

Trout are wary creatures, so you need to think in terms of their point of view, not yours. Contrary to popular belief, fish are not intelligent; however, they are instinctual and opportunistic. Internationally acclaimed author and angling expert Ernest Schwiebert contends, "We have been planting hatchery trout for the past century, in a mindless act of genetic pollution, until we have evolved fishermen who fail to understand that these are pale imitations of wild fish."

Wild trout look and behave far differently than their hatchery-raised cousins. For example, pen-raised fish tend to have large heads and slim bodies, and are not brightly colored. The concrete holding tanks and crowded conditions of the hatchery often cause their fins to have ragged edges. Until they become stream wise, stocked fish are not very selective. Because of the daily pellet feedings they receive, hatchery-raised fish will take almost any fly that is acceptably dressed and adequately presented. Conversely, wild trout have smaller heads, wider bodies and are brilliantly colored and marked. Wild trout are selective feeders and seem to jump more often and fight harder than stocked fish. Of paramount importance to the angler is the knowledge that hatchery raised fish do not flee immediately as do wild trout. This fact will directly affect how close you can get without frightening them. Therefore, it is important to develop proper wading skills like those discussed next in chapter eight, "Let's Go Fishing", and to understand the following information.

FIGURE 7.8

WHAT TROUT SEE

Beginners often look at this traditional "trout's window"[16] illustration and come away with the impression that this is all the fish sees (Figure 7.8). True, fish can see the outside world through Snell's Circle[17], called the window, but also be aware that trout see, hear and feel a great deal more below the surface. Professor Gary Borger explains, "Fish easily see everything around them under water, but have a very hard time seeing out of the water clearly. Distortion caused by refraction is the main problem, with distortion of distant objects and compressed images. This is the reason why fish are so afraid of things in the air, including fly lines. They are wary of objects that move quickly."

The fish's eye, with its powerful spherical lens, perfectly equips the trout to eat and avoid being eaten. The fish's eye is a marvelous and complex organ that can perform many functions at the same time. For example, the eye can scan for food and movement under water, and see food drifting on the surface and can watch for predators lurking outside its window all at the same time. Add to these facts that the mirror-like undersurface of the water surrounding the trout's window reflects all of the activity on the stream bottom yielding it still another perspective.

---

16. The window is defined by an approximate 97 degree cone with its apex at the fish's eyes and its base at the surface of the water. In essence, the cone of vision is a fish's periscope through which it sees out of the water.
17. Snell's Circle was named for the Dutch physicist Williebrord Snell, who first described the phenomenon in 1621.

This explanation may sound complicated, especially if you're new to the sport, so let's discuss what all this information means to the intelligent fly fisherman.

First

As you observe trout holding stationary in the water, be aware that refraction, the bending of light as it enters the water, causes the fish to appear closer to the surface yet farther away than their true position. This information will enable you to more accurately locate the fish and pinpoint your casts.

Second

There is a correlation between the trout's swimming depth under the water and the diameter of its window at the surface. The window diameter is approximately $2^1/_2$ times its depth. To illustrate this concept, a fish lying three inches beneath the surface, a typical surface feeding depth, will have a maximum window diameter at the surface of $7^1/_2$ inches. Figure 7.9 illustrates the outside world as the fish sees it. Notice how

FIGURE 7.9

compact and disjointed objects appear at the perimeter in comparison to the fly in the center of this picture which is in sharp focus. The closer the fish is to the surface the more distorted is its view of objects at the edge of the window. A trout lying close to the surface is usually clearly focused on food within inches of its snout. Therefore, you should be able to approach it more closely. However, your casts need to be accurate because of the narrow feeding lane. When moving into casting position, you should wade, kneel or crouch and cast sidearm, if necessary, to help eliminate movement visible to the trout.

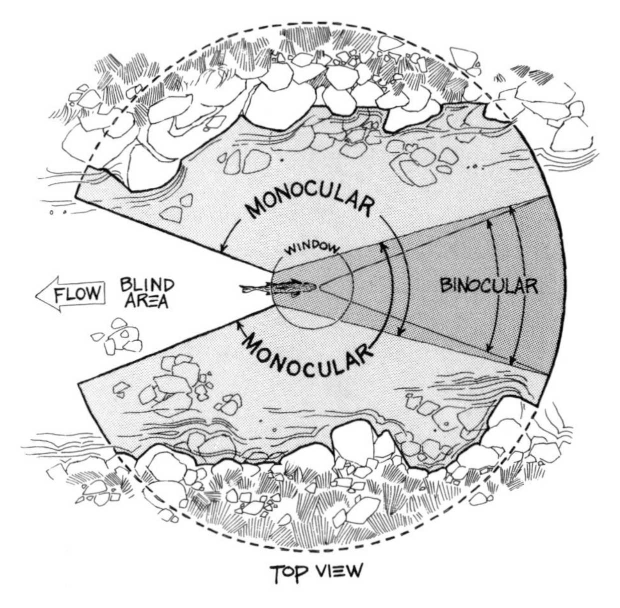

FIGURE 7.10

According to research done by authors, engineers and fly fishing enthusiasts Harmon and Cline[18], insects on the surface appear to be larger than they really are as the trout looks through its window. In essence, fish see your fly through a magnifying glass. Therefore, you must pay particular attention to the size of the naturals, and if you are going to err, do so with a smaller size fly. Remember, too, that any unnatural movement (drag) of your fly is amplified because of this magnification.

Third

Binocular vision, or the ability to focus both eyes on one subject, and the resulting field of view, is essential to provide the depth perception necessary for a trout to capture its food (Figure 7.10).

Internationally recognized fly fishing master John Goddard recently discovered new evidence that indicates the parameters of a trout's binocular vision are greater than conventionally thought[19]. The field of acute

18. Taken from the 1980 *Rod and Reel Magazine* article, "At the Edge of the Window," co-authored by Attorney Robert Harmon and Attorney John Cline.

19. Taken from the book, John Goddard's *Trout-Fishing Techniques*, pages 5-12.

binocular vision moves as the fish changes direction and can be as narrow and near as a few inches or as wide and far away as many yards; approximately 20 feet under ideal conditions. The trout's vision is affected by the water's clarity, current velocity and turbidity. Trout usually hold or return to a position to inspect and take food that drifts past them. In most cases, the deeper in the water trout are, the farther from a holding position they will move to intercept food. According to John Goddard, at increased depths of four to five feet, for example, "He [the fish] is unlikely to be concentrating through his binocular vision so everything on each side of his head within the 160 degree arc of his vision will be clearly seen to infinity."[20] Casting accuracy is not as important as a slow cautious approach without any sudden movement.

Most experts agree that all flies, but especially dry flies, should be presented to the side of a fish, if possible, rather than drifted directly over its head, in front of its snout or beyond. Trout usually concentrate their binocular vision in a relatively narrow lane. Therefore, casting accuracy is very important.

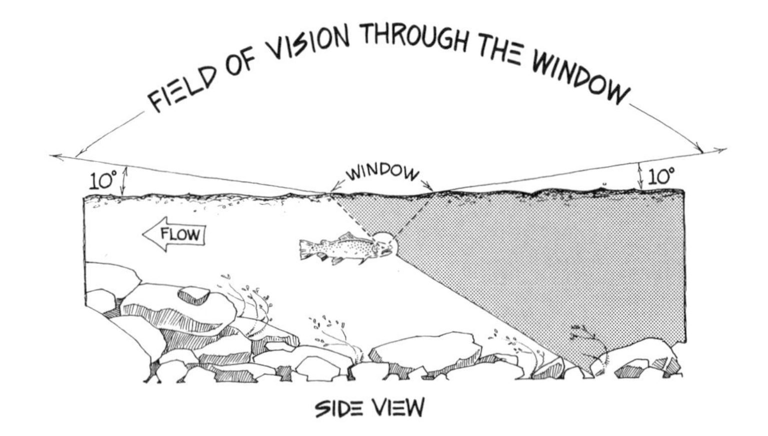

FIGURE 7.11

There is a 10 degree angle outside the water that extends up and away from the edge of the window. Little useful light enters the water below this level (Figure 7.11). Everything under that 10 degree line is invisible to the trout; however, any rapid movement like that produced by a moving fly rod or line can be briefly observed and possibly frighten the fish. This information is important to consider because if the banks are high, you may be better off kneeling and casting sidearm or approaching the fish by wading.

---

20. loc. cit., pages 6-12.

Fourth

The majority of what a trout sees is viewed with one eye only. This is referred to as monocular vision. This peripheral view starts forward at the 30 degree cone of binocular vision and extends all the way up and down and back to the 30 degree blind spot in the rear. This information is critical to the fisherman because a trout can visually detect motion everywhere. In effect, fish can see above, below, to both sides and behind at the same time. I would like to acknowledge and thank respected author Tom Rosenbauer for his illustration (page 12) in *Prospecting for Trout,* that highlights all that the fish sees. His drawing is one of the few that I know of that challenges anglers to think about everything the trout can see. With Tom Rosenbauer's

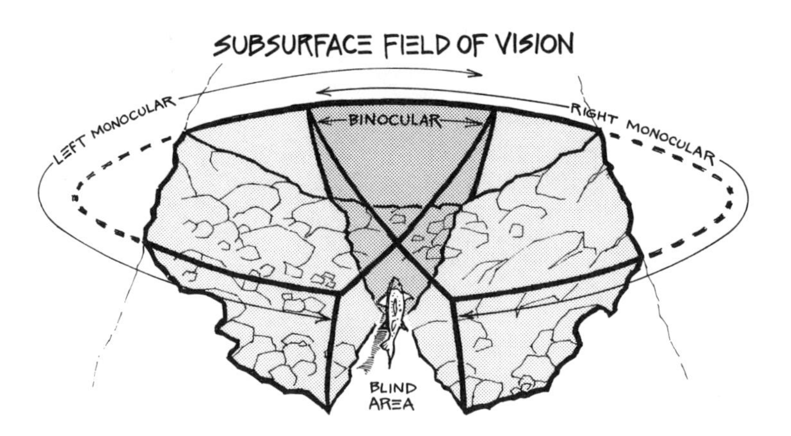

FIGURE 7.12a

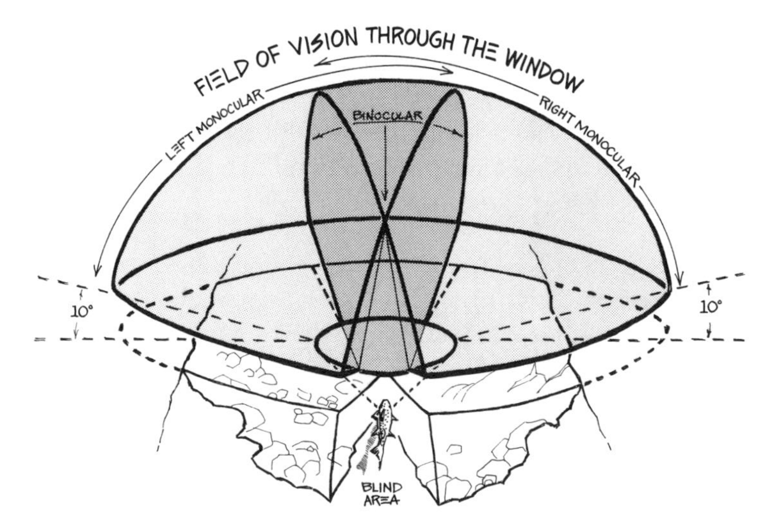

FIGURE 7.12b

kind permission, artist Jeff Wynn has redrawn the Rosenbauer illustration (Figure 7.12a) and added two others (Figures 7.12b and 7.12c) to further emphasize the extensive parameters of what a fish can see simultaneously in and out of the water.

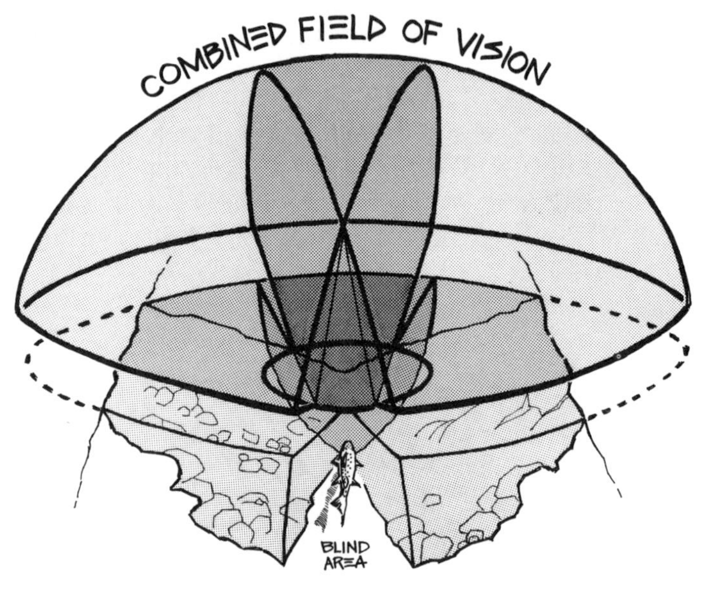

FIGURE 7.12c

Fifth

It is well documented that trout can detect color. According to author and fly fishing authority J. H. Fenner, "Fish see color almost exactly as humans do."[21] Red, orange and yellow, in that order, are most distinguishable to the fish, while green and blue are the least visible. This fact is significant because the color of your fly will need to approximate that of the insects the trout are feeding on. This is especially true when fishing in shaded areas away from direct sunlight. In addition, the color of your clothing, specifically your vest, shirt and hat, should blend in with the subtle tones of your surroundings.

Sixth

Trout have four blind spots. One is immediately above the head and the second is just in front of the snout. The third is under the body while the fourth extends in a 30 degree arc directly behind its tail. Traditional teaching has led us to believe that the size of the blind spot behind a trout usually affords fishermen the best opportunity to sneak up on the fish. This theory has been repeated so often that most anglers accept it as fact. I was no

21. Taken from the spring 1990 *Trout* magazine article, "Angling Optics," written by J. H. Fenner.

exception until Gary Borger corrected me. This premise is only partially true. Professor Borger informed me that the rear blind spot shifts because as Borger explained it, "The swimming motion of the fish allows it to see into the 30 degree blind spot to the rear. A fish sees there already, unless it's absolutely stationary, i.e., dead or catatonic."

With this in mind, what approach would give the fly fisherman the greatest opportunity for success? John Goddard contends, "Trout feeding at a depth of eighteen inches or so of the surface will most likely be concentrating through their binocular vision. Therefore, a better alternative would be casting from either side, opposite the trout, or from even slightly upstream of the fish's position. I am sure you will find he [the trout] is less likely to see you, but do remember to cast sideways and not overhead."[22]

Can Fish Smell And Hear?

All fish can smell, yet the refinement of this sense varies according to the species. For example, salmon travel thousands of miles through the boundless ocean, yet return to the river of their birth–guided in part by their nose. Smell helps trout find edible food, especially at night, and may contribute to their rejecting others. We also know at spawning time that smell aids the males in finding the gravid females. Armed with this information, it is important that suntan lotion, insect repellant or any other contaminate not be transferred by hand to our fishing flies.

Trout can hear and feel vibration long before they can see you. Therefore, you must walk or wade as quietly as possible. The hearing mechanisms of trout are well developed, and they can detect sound waves not only with their ears but also the lateral lines that run the length of their bodies on both sides. Trout are extremely sensitive to vibration to the extent that they can actually feel when other fish are moving. Gary Borger explained, "Sound waves that originate in the water travel three to four times faster than the same ones do in the air." Therefore, vibrations or noise like those caused by a heavy-footed or clumsy angler can easily frighten fish. This is why Tom Rosenbauer suggests that "you should walk and wade at a quarter of the speed that you think you should be moving!"

22. Taken from the book *John Goddard's Trout-Fishing Techniques*, pages 6-12.

20,000 Leagues Under The Sea

Fishing is not an escape from life, but often a deeper immersion into it, all of it, . . . the joyous and the miserable, the comic, the embarrassing.

– Harry Middleton

I have to paint this picture with words because, as you will discover, the photograph has been lost "20,000 leagues under the sea."

I truly believe that one of man's greatest gifts is his memory. Just think for a moment. What would you do without it?

I especially cherish my fishing memories. Some are truly delightful, while others are downright heartbreaking, but each is precious and tucked away safely for those cold winter nights. Unfortunately, as I grow older, it's becoming increasingly harder and more frustrating to recall all the good times I've been blessed with, so I record those moments on film.

For as long as I can remember, I have enjoyed using a camera, and I've surrounded myself with what I affectionately refer to as my "rogues' gallery," a collection of photos that I have taken, framed and hung in my office. They remind me every day of all the wonderful experiences I've enjoyed, the people I love, the places I have visited, and the adventures that I treasure.

I can vividly recall one golden Friday afternoon prior to the Saturday start of the inaugural Fly Fisherman's Symposium at Seven Springs Ski Resort in Champion, Pennsylvania. The trees seemed to explode with the vibrant colors of fall in striking contrast to the steel blue sky. My fishing buddies, Rich Roseborough and Earl Shapiro, and I decided to drive up early. We had shared a delicious lunch next to a pristine lake where two Canada geese had taken bread from our hands. The air was crisp and the autumn leaves falling from the trees floated gently then landed softly on the ground. The landscape resembled a Currier and Ives print. Rich exclaimed, "This is my favorite time of year."

I first met Rich Roseborough in the early 1980s while he was perched hundreds of feet in the air, welding the Neville Island Bridge that spans the Ohio River near Sewickley, PA. Passionate about fly fishing and by then tired of the dangerous work, Rich decided to open a fly fishing shop. Sixteen years later his business and fly fishing schools flourish. Rich is an accomplished caster, and he can stalk a trout stream and spot fish better than anyone I know. Rich also hand planes fine bamboo fly

Rich Roseborough

rods and makes classic fishing nets too. A master fly tier, Rich does a superb job of teaching others the art of tying flies, having taught classes at Allegheny Community College for years. He is witty and entertaining, and Rich truly loves people. I owe him my thanks because his confidence in my ability to help direct his fishing schools allowed me to perfect my instructional skills and spawned my desire to write this book. But back to the story…

When we had finished eating our lunch, the three of us decided to drive over to Laurel Run for a few hours of fishing. There wasn't much insect activity on stream that afternoon, but later, toward sunset, I couldn't get over the beauty of the scene as I watched Rich casting, the lowering sun accentuating his every move. Beams of light glistened off the varnish on his Jim Payne bamboo rod. I had to get a picture of it! I wound in my line, put the hook in the keeper, headed upstream and moved so quietly that Rich didn't even know I was there. Steadying myself against a huge boulder in the middle of the creek, I pulled out the new Olympus camera that I had received as a present for my birthday that July.

Rich casting reminded me of a scene from one of those classic swashbuckling films in which Errol Flynn brandished his sword while balancing on the yardarm.

To get a better angle for the shot, I started to crouch down in the water and move slowly toward the right bank when, Holy Mackerel! I dropped into a hole.

The last thing I remember was the cold "slap" from the chilly water. I finally surfaced and regained my footing some ten yards downstream. As I climbed out of the water, I caught the look of disbelief on Rich's face as he watched me emerge. I managed to save myself, but unfortunately, my brand new camera was lost "20,000 leagues under the sea," and so, too, the beautiful picture of Rich on that day.

Thankfully I had dry clothes to change into back at the truck. By the time Earl and Rich stopped fishing for the afternoon, the trees around the truck were festooned with wet, dripping clothes. To this day we still laugh about it, but I am sure they were glad it was I and not one of them who took the plunge.

LWYNN

Chapter Eight

Let's Go Fly Fishing

There are flyfishing writers eager to convince a readership that the sport is relatively simple, and it is helpful to simplify things for a new angler, but there is nothing simple about the full spectrum of fly fishing. It is a lifetime of pilgrimage and study.

– Ernest Schwiebert

One of the mistakes that I see a lot of people make when they get to their fishing destination is that they immediately gear up, run down to the water and start fishing. Consider the fact that you may have just driven for hours in a cramped, air-conditioned vehicle. Upon your arrival at the stream, take a few minutes to walk around and loosen up. Do some bending and stretching exercises. Stretching helps warm up your muscles which is especially important as we get older. Remember that fly fishing and its associated activities of casting, walking, climbing, kneeling and wading take some physical strength.

Yogi Berra, that great baseball personality of days gone by, wisely noted that "you can observe a lot just by watching." Orvis guide, Lori-Ann Murphy reminds us, "Even the best casters run out on the river and start fishing before they have assessed the situation." I suggest that rather than go straight to the water, take time to walk around and make some observations. For example, if there are any buildings, walkways or bridges close by, look for spider webs where you may find trapped insects that were flying near the stream that day or the night before. Another good place to look is near outdoor light fixtures. Insects tend to be attracted to light and subsequently they die from the heat given off by the bulb. Many may still be identifiable by species, size and color. As you walk to the stream, take a long look overhead and above the water, especially over the riffles, to see if there is any insect activity. Using binoculars or a monocular is helpful because you can keep your distance from the stream and not frighten any fish. Insects are usually drawn to streamside vegetation and can be uncovered by simply shaking the branches to see what falls or flies away. Finally, insects can often be found clinging to the underside of the leaves of trees and shrubs near the bank.

After ten minutes or so of observation, if no surface activity can be detected, chances are you are going to have to use some sort of subsurface fly or a top-water attractor pattern. A good way to determine what is going on under the surface is to turn over some of the submerged rocks close to the bank or in the riffle area of the stream to see what kind of nymphs may be under them. A compact pocket seine (a fine mesh screen) may be useful in collecting underwater or surface insects for on-the-spot identification. These may be the very ones the trout are taking. Try to match them with a pattern from your fly box or insect identification book. Acquaint yourself with the hatch charts that can be found in monthly fly fishing periodicals which are free at some fly tackle dealers, or from any of the excellent research books on sale there, too. These time-tested references are invaluable no matter how experienced you may be and should be consulted before making your fly selections. Doing so will ensure that before leaving home you have the right patterns for the time of year and the stream you are going to fish.

As I mentioned in the previous chapter, keep in mind that in addition to their keen sense of sight, fish are very attuned to vibration. As you walk close to the stream, keep a low profile and move as quietly as possible. Crawl if you must! Contrary to popular belief, the sound of your voice will not frighten fish because sound waves from outside the water travel much slower in the stream than in air, but remember that loud talking can annoy other anglers.

GEARING UP

Upon arriving at your fishing destination take your time gearing up. Routine can be your friend here. When you take a rod out of its tube, immediately replace the rod sack and tube cap. Assemble your rod carefully and align the guides as straight as possible. Never twist or screw the metal ferrules of a rod together. Metal ferrules must be pushed in straight. Graphite ferrules should be partially joined at least a quarter turn off line and then twisted and seated into final position. Make sure that the reel is attached with the handle on the correct side for either a left or right-hand wind. Secure the reel on the reel seat by either turning the locking mechanism tightly or by screwing the slide bands firmly onto the reel foot in a clockwise motion. This will ensure that the reel does not fall off during the course of the day's fishing.

To string the rod, find a grassy area, throw down a piece of carpet or your hat or rest the butt end of the rod on top of your boots to help keep sand and dirt out of the reel and the butt cap from getting scratched. Stringing can be expedited by doubling over the fly line and carefully threading it through every guide rather than trying to use the thin wispy end of the tippet (Figure 8.1). This practice virtually ensures that if the doubled line slips from your fingers, it will slide back only to the last guide rather than fall all the way down to the reel. Once the line is through the guides, straighten the leader by grasping and pulling it slowly through your fingers. The heat generated by the friction will straighten the nylon monofilament. I do not recommend using a rubber line straightener because it can stress the material. Last, tie on the fly and hook it in the keeper.

FIGURE 8.1

Never assemble your rod indoors, but if you must, always walk through a doorway with the rod tip ahead of you to avoid possible damage to it when the door closes behind you. The safest alternative is to have someone hold the door open for you.

Always keep your rod together with the fly tied on and hooked in the keeper while walking. Every now and then the ferrules may loosen during a day on stream, and your rod, if not held together by the hooked fly, could come apart. The worst scenario would be losing the tip section while walking in the dark and not discovering that it's missing until you get back to the car. If your rod does not have a hook keeper, you can simply slip the hook around the stripping guide. It is always a good idea to wear clear-lens glasses and use a flashlight or a Flex-lite® as you walk at night. You may also find it safer, especially when walking in the woods, to hold the grip in reverse with the rod tip extended behind you. This alternative almost guarantees that the tip section does not snag or break by hitting something that you cannot see in the dark. In addition, if you happen to stumble or fall, the rod will drop harmlessly behind you, thus avoiding the risk of your falling or stepping on your rod and breaking it. If you are walking with others, allow plenty of room between yourself and the person in front of or behind you, or walk abreast.

If you must leave your rod on the bank for any reason, do not lay it on the ground parallel to the water, especially in high grass near the edge. Instead, place the reel end in the grass with the top half of the rod extending out over the water. This placement will ensure that no one will accidentally step on it, and when you return, the rod will be easy to locate.

If you find it difficult to take your rod apart after your day onstream, you may need to use a pair of rubber gloves, rubber jar lid openers, or split rubber tubing to get a firmer grip. Hold the rod close to the ferrules with one hand on either side of the ferrule and pull, reversing the motion with which the rod was initially joined. Make sure nothing is around you that could possibly break the tip as it pulls apart and swings free. If this method does not work, get someone to help. Stand facing one another with the opposite ends of the rod between you, as if playing tug-o-war, and stagger your hands on each rod section near the ferrule and pull straight. If you do not take your rod apart after each day's use, the ferrules can be nearly impossible to separate. Try packing the ferrules in ice and allow them to chill for five minutes. Wipe off the moisture and hold the female ferrule for a half a minute or so. The heat from your hand may expand the female ferrule enough to allow the male ferrule to slide out easily. Never use pliers, a vice or hand tools to pull or pry ferrules apart! If you don't take your rod apart at night, it's important to store it safely indoors. After you wipe it off, you can either place it upright in a rod rack, or stand it behind a stationary object, preferably in the corner of your bedroom.

GETTING THE FLY ON THE WATER

Once you've attached your fly and tested the knot, the dry fly needs additional attention. Apply fly floatant sparingly to it and use the remainder to grease the leader from the tippet's connection knot back toward the fly line. Do not get floatant on the tippet. Be aware that the nail knot connecting the leader to the fly line tends to snag in the tip end. Therefore, it is important to manually pull that knot and a few feet of fly line through the top of the tip. To get the fly on the water or into the air, pull ten or fifteen feet of fly line from the reel, work it through the guides and flip the rod grip in a semicircular motion upstream. Release the fly and line and allow both to land on the water. Another technique is to rapidly false cast the rod while simultaneously attempting to get the line in the air by allowing it to run through the guides without hitting the water. However, this method does require some practice. When taking line from the reel, it is important to pull it out straight toward the tip, not down or to the side. This practice keeps the fly line from unnecessarily rubbing against the line guard and prematurely wearing out the line or guard. Once your fly and some of the line is on the water, lower the tip and continue to pull as much fly line from the reel as you will need. Wiggle the rod handle from side to side, pointing your rod downstream. Regardless of which technique you use, note the streamside vegetation and any possible obstructions up stream or down, overhead, and in front of you. Pay special attention to what is behind you. Being aware of these potential obstructions can persuade you to alter your casting direction or technique. Doing so may save you the frustration of snagging your fly.

THE INTERMEDIATE TARGET

Keep in mind that if you have more than one trout rising, it is always better to try to catch the one closest to you. This advice will help you avoid casting over rising trout, and in the event you hook a fish, the fight from the closest one will be less likely to alarm the remaining risers.

Once you see the fish that you want to catch, you should then proceed to cast to an intermediate target. The intermediate target is that imaginary spot a few feet in the air and three or four feet in front of the trout that forms a straight line between your fly and the fish's snout (Figure

FIGURE 8.2

8.2). Fly fishing differentiates itself from most other sports in that it has no boundary lines that act as a guide from you the angler, to your target, the fish. Therefore, when topwater dry-fly fishing, you need to create one. Remember that because the water is moving, by the time you see a rise form, it will appear to be downstream from the fish's true position. As a result, the trout will almost always be farther upstream from where you expect it to be.

If you are going to err, do so with a cast that is too short rather than too long. The trout may turn and come to your offering. At the very least you will not have frightened the fish with a bad cast or a line falling directly across its window or on top of its head.

THE STRIKE

When you see a trout rise to your dry fly on top of the water or feel a fish take your nymph or streamer under the surface, raise the rod tip in a smooth, deliberate motion to set the hook. Do not jerk the rod up violently. Such an overreaction may pull the fly out of the fish's mouth or break your delicate tippet. By a deliberate strike I mean quickly raise your wrist and forearm to bring the power of the rod tightly against the weight of the fish.

Ordinarily, trout do not attack a topwater dry fly with the same slashing fury that they take a subsurface streamer. Instead, a trout injests a dry fly with suction. This action is created by the fish opening its mouth first and then its gills, thus expelling water which draws the fly inside. It is important to have slack in your leader to avoid inadvertently pulling the fly out of the fish's mouth. This problem often occurs when using down-stream casting techniques. A delayed hook set almost ensures that the fish has time to close its mouth, making a secure hookup more likely.

THE FIGHT IS ON!

When fishing with the line on the water, the middle finger that holds the fly line in your rod hand should be slightly more relaxed than the rest of the fingers that are holding the grip. When you set the hook and play the fish, that middle finger tightens again as you either give line, strip line in or hold the rod in front of you. Getting the feel of each one of these hand positions comes with time, so the best advice I can give is to get out and go fishing! The experience of casting, fishing and landing fish will be invaluable in learning how much pressure you can apply to your tackle without breaking the line and losing the fish.

Once you hook a trout, don't be alarmed if other fish rush toward the one that you have caught. It is a natural predatory reaction to a fish in distress. Some time during your fishing adventures you will either hear of, or experience, a "foul-hook." The term foul-hook is used to designate a fish that has been snagged somewhere other than its mouth. A foul-hooked trout usually fights harder and invariably feels bigger than it actually is.

When fighting a fish with a graphite rod, hold the rod in the conventional position with your rod hand comfortably in front of your chest, the rod tip elevated and extended up and away at the one o'clock position and with the reel facing down. You should get the slack line onto the reel as soon as possible. You can accomplish this by trapping the line in your rod hand between the middle finger of your rod hand and the grip. Drape the slack line over the little finger of your rod hand, placing tension on the line (Figure 8.3). Now quickly and neatly wind the excess line onto the reel. Maintain constant pres-

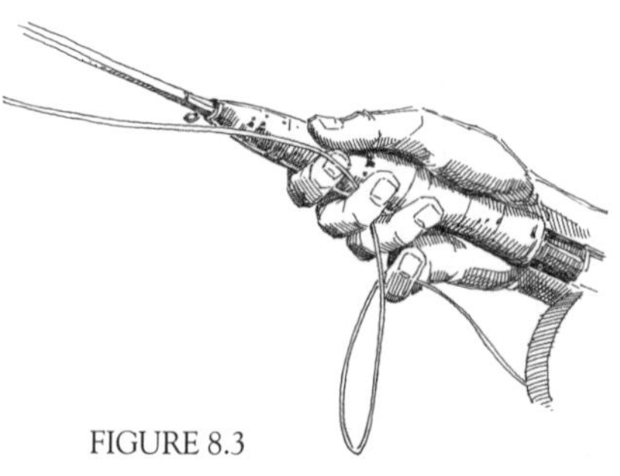

FIGURE 8.3

sure on the fish while winding line onto the reel. As you wind, turn the reel handle smoothly and space the line evenly across the entire surface of the spool to avoid jamming the line up on one side. If the fish makes an unexpected run, the line will come off the reel quickly and trouble free.

If you need to strip line in while standing on the bank, you should make every effort to try to drop the fly line onto the shorter grass and not into high weeds or mud. Obviously, you'll want to avoid stepping on your fly line, too. If you are wading and casting upstream, pull the stripped-in line around the line hand side of your body. You will then know exactly where the line is at all times and avoid tangles. If you are fishing downstream, the current will keep the line conveniently in front of you. An effective alternative to retrieve excess fly line is to make three coils in your line hand as you retrieve. This technique is described in Joan Wulff's book, *Joan Wulff's Fly Casting Techniques* pages 118-119, and is a useful skill to learn.

A hooked fish will normally look for cover to hide under. If you still have slack line between your rod hand and the reel, trap the line between your middle finger and the grip, while simultaneously holding your rod tip at one o'clock and pointing it in the direction that the fish is running. Allow the fish to take the excess line smoothly and with gentle pressure until the slack is gone. By turning the entire rod (like a windshield wiper) to the left or the right, you may be better able to control the fish and keep it from making long runs. If the trout takes a long run up or down the stream or jumps into the air, give it some slack by lowering the rod tip, thus easing the rod pressure on the fish. Doing so may cause the fish to stop or turn, allowing you to catch your breath and re-evaluate your strategy.

If the fish runs toward you, you will have to move quickly: get the rod up in front of you, trap the line under the middle finger of your rod hand and strip in the line to keep pace with the fish until it stops or turns in another direction. The most efficient place to hold the rod when fighting a fish is directly in front of your chest. This position is comfortable and allows you to better control the rod and the line. Do not fight a fish with your hands held above your head unless special circumstances require it. Otherwise, it is needlessly tiring and accomplishes nothing.

WADING

Wading can be the most enjoyable and productive way to fly fish. Getting into the water allows you to get closer to the fish, and because you will make shorter casts, your casts will be more accurate, helping you eliminate the troublesome problems of drag. A poorly executed back cast is less likely to become snagged on an obstruction. In addition, the cool water feels great in hot weather.

It is important to know and follow the general guidelines for safe and effective wading. Harry Murray feels that "careful wading is one of the most important skills a beginner must learn." Slipping or tripping on underwater rocks, logs or other obstructions is always a possibility when wading, even for veteran anglers. As we discussed in chapter one, the probability of such a dunking is inevitable, making the inclusion of a change of clothes and a bath towel in your fishing gear quite mandatory. It happens to everyone so be prepared.

Streams vary dramatically. While some are easily negotiated, others are downright treacherous because of slippery or rocky stream bottoms. The best advice I can give to you is, "If you can't swim, you shouldn't wade." The most important piece of wading equipment you can use is your brain, so think before you step in. Most accidents happen when you make a hasty decision or a sudden, uncalculated move. Remember, clear water, especially water that is clear to the bottom, is invariably deeper than it appears. If a stream looks deep or dangerous, then it usually is! The worst falls occur in shallow water because there is no cushion between you and the rocky bottom. A tumble into deep water can be embarrassing, but a fall into shallow water can injure you and damage your tackle.

If you are going to fish in water that you have never visited before, it is important to find out in advance what the water conditions are, including its bottom characteristics. You may discover, for example, that wading is prohibited in the particular stream where you plan to fish. Remember, knowing what others simply overlook or think is nonessential will help make you a more intelligent angler.

It is always safer to use a wading staff and stream cleats if you are the least bit uncertain about a stream's wading conditions. Wading staffs are made of wood or collapsible aluminum and are used like a walking stick for balance. Stream cleats are like "tire chains" for your boots. They offer a better grip on slippery surfaces. As you move through the water, stream cleats will give you better footing, and the wading staff will enable you to feel your way ahead with greater confidence. Attach the wading staff's bungee cord to your wader belt or the "D" ring on your vest so that it will not drift away while you are fishing. Do not forget your polarized sun glasses. They will also increase your visibility. All these accessories work in concert to keep you from falling and harming yourself or damaging your tackle.

Clumsy, noisy wading frightens fish. Therefore, it is imperative that you move as quietly as possible while in the water. When you approach a stream, enter where the water is shallow and the current is slow. Sometimes the most difficult part of wading is getting out of the mud. Mud can accumulate near the banks and in slower moving areas like backwaters and eddies. If you get stuck, twist your foot slightly as you slowly lift it. This movement should break the suction and free your boot or wading shoe. If you encounter mud that is so deep you cannot get out, do not panic. In that case either call for help from someone nearby, or unfasten your wader straps and wading belt and swim out of the mud. Caution is the key word when climbing around slippery banks and on large, wet, or moss covered rocks. Be aware, too, that snakes could be out sunning themselves, so keep your eyes open and be alert to avoid an unpleasant encounter.

Take your time. Evaluate the conditions before you get into the water. You may find it safer to sit down on the bank and slide into the water feet first. Once you are in the water, stop to catch your breath. This break will allow any surface disturbance you may have created when climbing in to dissipate. It will also allow you some time to think about where you want to go, as well as to observe any rising trout that may be nearby. Last, if you have inadvertently frightened any fish, waiting a few minutes may give them the time and confidence to return to their holding positions.

Stealth is the key when moving about in the water. Ernest Schwiebert is convinced that "stealth is still our most important skill. Wild trout stubbornly retain the poetic grace we call wildness and they must be stalked before we can capture them." Try to maintain as streamlined a profile as you can. To achieve this simply turn your body sideways to the flow and move forward slowly one step at a time. Remember to lift your lead foot (the foot you move first) slightly as you step forward while feeling ahead with your wading staff. Always take short steps, searching ahead with your toe first. After your lead foot has obtained a firm and secure purchase, you may safely bring your anchor foot forward. Remember that the anchor foot should never cross over the lead foot. Avoid larger obstacles by going around them, not over them. It is important to move deliberately, stopping periodically to allow the water to calm down, reevaluate the conditions and make any necessary adjustments to your tackle or approach.

Safety is also an important consideration when it is time to get out of the water. It is vitally important to find a shallow point near the edge where you can climb out and onto the bank without slipping. I recommend further that you never grab hold of anything to help pull yourself out of the water unless you are absolutely certain of its stability. This advice may save you the embarrassment of falling in backwards and will, once again, help you avoid the ever-present danger of injuring yourself or breaking your rod and reel. If you cannot find a safe spot to get out of the water, just return to where you got in. Turning around in a stream can be challenging especially if the water is deep and the current is fast. In this case, you can maintain control by turning slowly, taking short steps and planting each foot carefully.

The easiest place to cross a stream is at the top of a riffle. The footing is usually firm, the water shallow, and the current slow. If you are having difficulty crossing a stream, pick out a target on the opposite bank across and down stream that is diagonal to the flow. Move slowly, yet deliberately and, if necessary, rest in the pocket water behind any large obstruction. If you lose your footing in deep water, do not panic. Try to float feet first until the current brings you to shallow water where you can get out safely. Save yourself first and worry about your tackle later.

BARBLESS HOOKS

There have been some fascinating and informative articles written lately that discourage the use of barbless hooks.[23] For the past 15 years, our instructors have advocated their use for three reasons.

First, on an increasing number of streams the law requires the use of barbless hooks and a substantial fine may be imposed if you are caught not using them. Second, it has been my experience that trout are not lost due to using a barbless hook. To keep the hook from working loose you must maintain constant pressure on the fish. Third, many biologists throughout the United States contend that barbless hooks are safer to use. A barbless hook is more easily and less painfully removed from the skin or clothing. This may save you a trip to the local emergency room or prevent damage to an expensive piece of clothing.

The following removal technique, which was devised in the early nineteen 1960s by Australian physician Dr. Theo Cooke, works the first time, every time. However, it cannot be performed alone.

1. Double over a 20 inch piece of 2X, or stronger, monofilament.

2. Loop the monofilament around the bend of the embedded hook and hold all ends firmly and securely in one hand.

3. With the opposite hand, press the hook eye and shank down into the skin. With the hand holding the monofilament, simultaneously snap the hook at its bend up and out, removing the hook. I emphasize snapping the loop hard and quick.

4. Wash the wound thoroughly with soap and water, treat it with antiseptic and dress it with a sterile bandage. If pain persists or the wound becomes swollen, inflamed or infected, go to a healthcare professional for immediate treatment.

---

23. There is new research which states that barbless hooks may tear the lining of the fish's mouth because the hooks do not set immediately. Consequently, they can dislodge easily and move around, damaging more tissue before finally setting. The researcher believes that those hooks that do penetrate do so more deeply and cause more damage, particularly in larger hook sizes or in smaller fish. This information, however, has not changed what we teach our students. Simply put, our instructors believe the benefits of using barbless hooks far outweigh these unsubstantiated liabilities.

UNSNAGGING A FLY

With one exception, never use your rod as a lever to dislodge a snagged fly. Using a rod this way places too much strain on it and could loosen the guides or scratch or break the rod. In addition, you also run the risk of being seriously injured by the graphite splinters.

There are many techniques that you can use to effectively dislodge a snagged fly. The first would be to firmly hold the rod grip and point the rod directly at the snag, eliminating any tension on the rod. With your line hand, pull slowly but firmly to see if the fly will easily free itself. Safety dictates that you look away as you pull to protect your eyes, especially if you're not wearing glasses. If the fly comes free, it could easily snap back and hit you in the face. Second, if the snag is within a rod's length of you, strip in all the line and leader and carefully use the tip end to push and dislodge the snag. This exception is the only time when it is safe to use your rod. If this technique does not work, you may find it more effective to point the rod at the fly, put tension on the line and leader, and then snap the line back by releasing it quickly. If you're still unsuccessful, try the following method which is particularly helpful when a streamer, wet fly or nymph has become snagged on the stream bottom. Pull some line from the reel and grasp it tightly against the handle of the rod. You should have enough slack line to do a roll cast. With the rod tip pointed at eleven o'clock, the upper roll cast position, smartly roll cast in the direction of the snag. As the loop of line passes the snagged fly, it will often reverse the pull on the hook point and may free the fly. If these methods fail, point the rod directly at the snagged fly, turn your face away, close your eyes, and pull the line until the tippet snaps. Do not wade over to retrieve the fly. Doing so will only frighten the very fish you've been trying to catch.

When beginners snag their fly line or rod due to a poorly executed cast, they invariably attempt to cast the snagged fly free or continuously flip the rod in a circle, tangling the line and making a bad situation even worse. It is always better to stop as soon as you detect the slightest trouble and correct the problem by hand.

One Of Us Has To Go!

It must, of course, be admitted, that large stories of fishing adventure are sometimes told by fisherman—and why should that not be so? Beyond all question there is no sphere of human activity so full of strange and wonderful incidents as theirs.

– President Grover Cleveland

You'll never meet anyone who likes people more than I do. I enjoy watching them, interacting with them and, most of all, teaching them to fly fish! Our schools and the hundreds of students who have attended them over the years have been delightful.

I consider fly fishing to be one of the ultimate one-on-one challenges yet some people try to turn it into an outdoor social. Fly fishing for trout was never intended to be a spectator sport or a team event. Please don't misunderstand me; there are occasions when you will want companionship, but for the most part, the thrill of catching fish is heightened when you are alone.

The anticipation, preparation and responsibilities associated with conducting a weekend fly-fishing school for two dozen people are almost overwhelming. Once the students start to arrive, my time is not my own. Recognizing this fact, Rich Roseborough planned long ago that the instructors would have the Cottage section of Spruce Creek to ourselves on Friday afternoons.

Despite my affection for people, I must confess that I covet those quiet hours. Just me, the fish and the expectation of catching one. It's truly a time that I consider sacred.

One Friday afternoon a few summers ago after Rich, Earl and I unloaded all the food and supplies at the Cottage, I geared up and headed off to the upper section of the stream. I sat on the stone near the Willow Pool to see if any fish were rising.

For as long as I can remember the Willow Pool has been one of the most productive, challenging and insect-rich sections on Spruce Creek. It's a magical place where all the elements that make up prime trout habitat coincide. A towering willow tree nearly five feet wide has grown up and out into the water, separating the upper and lower sections. Much of the pool is sheltered by the canopy of leaves, and trout flourish within the labyrinth of submerged branches and underwater roots. In the upper section, a hillside of ash, maple and dogwood trees rises above the far bank protecting the fish from direct sunlight and winged predators. Two huge logs lie near each bank opposite one another. A sprawling multi-flora rose bush has grown up next to the water on the far bank just upstream from the willow. Its limbs extend over and into the water forming a tunnel that invites trout into its protective lie. A massive boulder protrudes through the surface twenty feet upstream of the willow. It slows the current and heads a channel that extends 50 feet downstream under the willow and into the lower section. Hungry trout in this beat sip midges and small mayflies near the far bank under the sheltering

limbs of sumac, elm and other riparian vegetation. The water surface is as smooth as glass and requires a slow, cautious approach when wading. Finally, there is a bench-like stone near the willow tree that has become a landmark. It calls out to every fisherman passing by to sit for a while and think trout.

Nothing was happening below, but along the far bank in the stretch just upstream, I could see a huge fish lying near the edge. Rather than wade in and risk spooking it, I crawled slowly, staying low to the ground, pausing briefly only to reconfirm that the fish was still there. Arriving at my casting position near the bank, I knelt in the dew-covered grass, my backside resting against my boot heels. I breathed a sigh of relief as my nose filled with the sweet smell of spearmint. I could make out the silhouette of what appeared to be a 20-inch brown trout, lying tight against the log along the far bank. I tied on my trusty Steinhart Beetle, tested the knot and pulled out just the right amount of line. I had to false cast sidearm to avoid the over hanging limbs.

Suddenly, out of the corner of my eye, I caught the movement of something downstream, about 100 yards away, moving in my direction. I stopped casting to get a better look. From 75 yards away it looked like a huge cat frolicking carelessly along the bank. At 50 yards, I knew it was no feline because I could make out its elongated body and porpoise-like motion. For a moment, I thought that someone's pet ferret was loose, but it was too large to be that! I knew that whatever it was, it saw me, too, and at 30 yards away, it was closing in fast! At 20 yards the intruder had a "this-creek-isn't-big-enough-for-the-two-of-us" look on its face. At 15 yards, it became apparent that I was in its way, and one of us had to go! I immediately jumped to my feet, wound in the fly line, put the hook in the keeper and stood my ground.

Instantly, the critter slowed down. As we stared at one another, I realized it was an otter. Its wet brown coat glistened in the sunlight, and the gray bristly hairs around its muzzle stood out in contrast. It was beautiful! The interloper continued creeping toward me slowly, and for a moment I was incapable of moving or breathing. I thought about using my fly rod to discourage its advance, but when I saw its sharp teeth, and lots of them, I decided those choppers would make short work of my bamboo rod.

The darn thing was almost at my feet, so I cautiously leaned over to pick up a stick. The move startled my uninvited guest, and immediately it dove head first into a nearby hole. Unfortunately for it, the convenient hideaway was too small. The back half of the creature's body, including those big webbed feet and long thick tail, stuck straight up in the air, kicking and twisting for all it was worth. What a Kodak moment! I had to get a picture of it, so I quickly reached into my vest pocket only to discover that I had left my camera in the truck. The guys would *never* believe my story. I had the beast just where I wanted him, and for a fleeting moment I actually considered grabbing the varmint by its tail, pulling it from the burrow and taking it back to the cottage. "Are you out of your mind?" I thought. "What a stupid idea!" I decided to leave well enough alone and beat a hasty retreat.

At dinner, when I told everyone about my afternoon adventure, they reacted just as I had expected they would. "You had to much to drink," or "You must have stayed out in the sun too long, Tom," they laughed.

Chapter Nine

Catch And Release

A good game fish is too valuable to be caught only once.
The fish you release is your gift to another angler.

– Lee Wulff

If you truly want to kill stocked trout, and it is permitted, you shouldn't let instructors like me make you feel guilty about doing so. After all, fishermen spend a lot of time and money purchasing tackle, buying a license and a trout stamp and traveling to the stream. To subdue a creature that is lesser than we, then kill it, cook it and eat it is an act, for some, that satisfies their predatory instincts and is very natural. Michael T. Brett Ph. D. suggests, "Sometimes killing a few fish can improve a fishery."[24]

However, there is another side to this story that I want you to consider. If anglers kept every trout they caught, especially wild fish, there would soon be too few left. This fact is one obvious reason why there are increasingly more rules and regulations governing catch limits to ensure that there will be plenty of fish to catch for all of the people who participate in this sport.

As for me, I can't explain why releasing trout unharmed makes me feel so good; it just does. I find something magical in that special moment after I have admired the fish when I hold it into the current, feel its strength come back and watch it swim away. I feel great knowing that there may come a day when someone else may experience the pleasure of catching it again. That someone could be you or, for that matter, me!

Over 60 years ago, the late Lee Wulff wrote "To be caught only once" in his 1938 book *Handbook of Freshwater Fishing.*

---

24. From the magazine, *Fly Fisherman,* February 1998 issue, pages 18-28.

> *"It is a long step from the day that the fisherman's catch meant life and health to himself and his family, to our present day, where anglers fish for sport alone. Even the day of the fisherman who consistently hangs up his trophies of the day to brag about is passing. Pride in accomplishment will always remain. But, seemingly, angling is reaching a new high plane when fishermen can spend the day on the lake or stream catching fish, returning them to the water unharmed, and come home empty-handed. That angler keeps no trophies to show his fellow men as proof of his prowess, but contents himself with the pleasure of a day well spent in the surroundings he loves. He has fished for sport and not for glory; upon him and those who follow his leadership, the future of angling depends."*

These sentiments are still as true today as they were then. Maybe more so.

My challenge to you is this: the next time you catch a fish, let it go. You will have a memory that will last a lifetime and the satisfaction of sharing a precious, limited resource.

How To Handle And Release Your Fish Unharmed

Bear in mind that a fish, regardless of its size, is virtually weightless in the water. In addition, its body is designed to function in that watery environment. When you take a fish out of water, it is traumatized by rough handling, a lack of oxygen, a change in air pressure and temperature and fear. It is easier on the fish if it is landed close to the bank and kept in the water. You will want to lead its head toward the edge of the water where the current is not moving swiftly or the water is not as deep. Once the trout is in calmer water, be sure to kneel, if necessary, when removing the hook and releasing the trout. Fish will generally flop around, and if you drop one, there is less likelihood of harming it if it is held close to the water surface. Be extra careful with a fish on the bank. It's very easy to drop one on the ground and possibly hurt it, often with fatal consequences.

Keep your hands wet when handling a trout. Cradle large fish with one hand, under its "chin," directly behind its mouth, and with the other hand around its "wrist," directly in front of the tail. The rib cage of a fish angles upward acutely an inch or so back from its chin. If you grasp its belly, especially when holding a heavier fish, its own unsupported weight can actually crush some of its delicate internal organs. You can even fracture its vertebral column. Never squeeze a fish for the same reason, and do not lift a trout by its tail or lower jaw. Many of the aforementioned reasons apply here, too. In addition, you will also avoid its very sharp teeth.

Trout have a slippery mucus coating their scales that reduces friction and allows the fish to slip through the water effortlessly. Overhandling a fish, especially with dry hands, or netting a fish can remove some of this coating and make the fish more susceptible to bacteria and disease. Therefore, I recommend not using a net when landing a fish if at all possible. If you feel that the situation requires using a net, keep the net and the trout in the water, lift the hoop of the net high enough to expose the head of the trout only, and with your other hand, use a hemostat to remove the hook. It is important to keep a fish in the water as much as possible. If you can avoid it, do not remove the fish from the water at all. Otherwise, make its time out of water brief, ideally ten to fifteen seconds at the most. This greatly reduces the possibility of injury or death.

Before you remove the hook from the fish's mouth, pull out some extra fly line from the reel to relieve any tension on the leader and hook. Tuck the rod firmly under your arm and keep the tip elevated so that when you bend over or kneel down to release the fish, you do not inadvertently jam the tip end into the bank or the rocky stream bottom.

If the hook is too deep inside the fish's mouth or it is hard to remove, simply cut off the fly as close to the hook eye as possible. Over the course of a month or so the hook will either dislodge on its own, or eventually dissolve. Remember, if you must handle the fish, wet your hands prior to taking it out of the water. If the fish is too big for one person to handle, you may find it necessary to have another angler help net the fish or remove the hook.

If a smaller trout of 12 inches or less flops around, try turning it upside down, cradling the dorsal fin in your hand. This position disorients the fish, and it may lie still. With your opposite hand, take a hemostat and remove the hook. If that is not possible, cut the leader close to the hook eye and let the fish go.

Fish will expend all their energy to resist being caught. Therefore, once you have removed the hook and are ready to release the fish, keep it in shallow water near the bank. Cradling it as described, hold the fish upright and point it face forward into the current. Allowing the water to run through its mouth and out the gills will revive it. When you feel the fish's energy and strength come back, uncradle its chin, release the wrist and let it swim way.

New research from the University of Florida indicates that a fish kept out of water for 60 seconds or more has a mortality rate twice as high as a fish kept out of the water for half that time. Therefore, if you wish to admire or take a picture of your catch, keep it in the water, cradle it gently and kneel down so that if it does fall when you lift it, the fish will not get hurt. If you plan to photograph your catch, have the person who is going to take the picture set the focus and exposure before you pick up the fish. For those of you who routinely display your catch alongside your rod on the bank, please reconsider your actions. Such displays are traumatic to the fish.

If you are going to release trout, and I hope you will, it is every fly fisherman's responsibility to learn how to release them unharmed. In the March 1995 issue of *Fly Fisherman* magazine an article written by Patrick Trotter Ph.D. titled "Hooking Mortality of Trout" examines this subject thoroughly. Doctor Trotter, a respected author and fishery science consultant, studied nearly 20 scientific papers on this subject. Based on his research, he concluded that: (1) trout caught on flies had a slightly higher rate of survival than fish caught on lures and a significantly higher survival rate than those caught on bait because trout tend to ingest live bait deeper. In addition, removing live bait is more injurious to the fish; (2) fish caught on barbless hooks suffer lower hooking mortality than those caught on barbed hooks. Barbless hooks are more easily removed and cause less trauma to the fish; (3) trout hooked in the jaw or "lips" had a higher rate of survival than those hooked in the tongue, the eyes, or the roof of the mouth. Trout hooked in the gills or esophagus/stomach had the lowest survival rate of all; and (4) trout that are deeply hooked stand a much better chance of survival if the tippet is cut and the fish is released. Studies revealed that most of the hooks that were left in the fish either dissolved or dislodged on their own without harming the fish. Finally, Doctor Trotter mentioned to me that the use of a stomach pump, an instrument that resembles a cooking baster and is used to extract the contents from a trout's esophagus for immediate identification, in the best of hands is still traumatic and dangerous to the fish. Therefore, I discourage its use by anyone, but especially someone that is new to the sport.

If during the revival process the trout's body starts to turn "belly up," it is suffering from acute oxygen deprivation and a buildup of lactic acid. This condition often occurs when the fish has been overplayed or kept out of the water too long. Immediately right the fish, hold it face forward into the current and gently move it forward and back. This technique is especially helpful in still or slowly moving water. If, after five minutes or so, the fish still hasn't revived, quickly take it out into heavy current, preferably behind a sheltering obstacle, and hold it face first into the stronger current. The higher concentration of oxygen in the stronger current should revive it.

There is little that is more heartbreaking to the responsible angler than seeing a dead fish floating down a favorite trout stream. Learn and practice the proper technique to revive and release a fish unharmed.

If you catch the trophy of a lifetime and wish to preserve it beyond a photograph, you should be aware of a new and exciting technique that gives you a beautiful mount without sacrificing the fish. A skilled taxidermist can produce a life-size fiberglass reproduction of your catch based on an original photograph and description.[25a/b] You might contact your local fly shop to see if they offer this service or know someone who does.

A unique service advertised in *Fly Fisherman* Magazine will reproduce a photograph of your fish using a hand watercolor technique. The rendering includes the vital statistics of the catch documented in professional calligraphy beneath the portrait.[26]

A full size three-dimensional wood carving of your catch is also available, and it is simply magnificent. It, too, has all the vital statistics of your catch hand painted on the mounting board below the carving.[27]

Finally, you can release your fish but keep the memory of the catch with an original full-dimensional wood carving and habitat done by Artist John Zeiselmeier who will personally sculpt your trophy in stunning detail from a photo and description. This life-size carving is truly a beautiful alternative to traditional taxidermy.[28a/b]

25a. Andres Taxidermy
2950 Outlaw Drive
Belgrade, Montana 59714
1 (406) 388-7226

25b. Mike Moss - B.C. Wildlife Studios
4701 Argonaut Road - Campbell River
British Columbia, Canada VPH1P3
1(250) 286-1214

26. Trout Portraits
P.O. Box 1502
Billings, Montana 59103-1502
1 (800) 353-0055

27. Dr. Peter Lyne
Rintein: Borrowfield Close
Hove, Sussex BN3 6 TP
England 01144273507328

28a. John Zeiselmeier
6 Fenton Lane
Bordertown, New Jersey 08505
1 (609) 298-6800

28b. Ellen McCaleb
308 Bridge Street
Phoenixville, PA 19460
(610) 917-1315

"LEFTY"

Lefty Kreh, by far the greatest of them all.
– Ed Jaworowski

While wandering through the exhibit hall at the inaugural Fly Fisherman's Symposium at Seven Springs Ski Resort in Champion, Pennsylvania, I heard a collective sigh of "ohs" and "ahs" coming from behind a partition. I poked my head around the corner to see what all the commotion was about. There, in the middle of a standing-room only crowd, stood a man demonstrating the art of fly casting. Though I'd read all of Lefty's books and magazine articles, he didn't look at all as I had envisioned him. As I stood awestruck, Lefty effortlessly picked up what seemed to be 50 feet of fly line in only one cast. With the line in mid air, the mesmerized crowd watched as he took the rod apart and continued to cast with the tip section alone. When Lefty finished, the applause was deafening.

Later that morning I waited in line for an hour just to meet him. When we finally met, his handshake was confident and his voice warm. His contagious smile made me feel as if I had known him forever. Unfortunately, I was taking up too much of his time, and the line of people waiting behind me went clear out the door. Lefty graciously gave me his phone number and invited me to call. Since that first meeting, I've kept up a long distance phone relationship with him, and I have grown to know and admire him.

Bernard Victor Kreh was born in 1925 in Frederick, Maryland, a sleepy farming town in the western part of the state. His father died tragically in the early 1930s leaving three sons, a daughter and a wife. To say that the family was devastated would be an understatement. Their situation was so desperate that they had to go on welfare to survive. As the oldest son, Lefty was thrust into the position of being the man of the house. To help make ends meet his mother took in laundry, and Lefty started catching and selling catfish to pay his way through high school. Lefty became so successful at his fishing business that he brought home more money than all his young friends, and he even earned more than some older men with full-time jobs. Thus began Lefty's 60-year love affair with fish and fishing.

Lefty got his nickname while playing basketball at Frederick High. Lefty is ambidextrous, and when he dribbled down court, he would often look right, fake everyone out, including some of his teammates, then shoot left-handed and score.

During World War II, Lefty earned five battle stars and was awarded the Purple Heart. He did tell me, "One of the happiest days of my life was when I got discharged!" In 1945 while home on furlough, he met Evelyn Mask and married her a year later. Ev, as her friends call her, seems to be unimpressed with Lefty's celebrity status. She told me, "I just let him go off and do his thing." Lefty taught her to fish, but she admitted, "I can only do it for an hour or so and then I lose interest."

Evelyn explained, "Lefty had always wanted to be a game warden because he really enjoyed hunting and was pretty good at it." As a matter of fact, she told me, "Lefty put on shooting demonstrations for the Remington Arms Company," but after the war he took a job as the night foreman at the Army Biological Warfare Laboratories at Fort Detrich, Maryland. "The job was perfect for me," Lefty recalled, "because I spent most of the days huntin' or fishin'." Lefty's journalism career started when he began writing the outdoor column for the *Frederick News Post,* and he attributes most of his writing success to his long-time friend and mentor, the late Joe Brooks. During that two-year period, his popularity expanded to include syndication in a dozen newspapers. He even had his own television show in Baltimore. "A staff photographer helped me learn to use a 35mm camera when few outdoor writers were doing that," Kreh said. Lefty became so accomplished as a photographer that he taught nature photography for the National Wildlife Federation for nearly ten years. In 1964 he moved to Florida to run the world's largest fishing tournament, the Metropolitan South Florida Fishing Tournament based in Miami. In the early 1970s, Lefty took a writing job at the *St. Petersburg Times* but moved back to Maryland within a year. Once back home he became the outdoor columnist for the *Baltimore Sun* and retired from the paper in 1989.

Today his interests are centered around photography, writing, editing, making public appearances, giving casting lessons and answering the stacks of mail that seem to accumulate overnight. He has a darkroom that would rival Kodak's finest, and it may not surprise you to learn that he has designed photographic equipment and pioneered better techniques to take and develop photographs. Lefty is also an innovative and accomplished fly tier, but he once confessed, "There just doesn't seem to be enough time in the day." This statement comes from a man who sleeps only five hours a night. As fly casters go, Lefty has few equals, but what distinguishes him is his ability to teach others by example. Lefty can demonstrate a student's mistake using either hand. He has a fantastic sense of humor, is quick with a joke and always makes time to help others.

Lefty has a real soft spot for kids and is willing to spend time with them whenever he can. Once while at a large outdoor show in California, Lefty was being introduced to a packed house. As he walked down the aisle toward the casting pool, he noticed a little boy about five-years-old standing there crying. Lefty immediately stopped, knelt down and asked the boy if he was lost. The child shook his head "yes," and Lefty, without hesitation, handed his rod to someone in the crowd, took the youngster into his arms and headed straight to the security office. Respected fly tier D. L. Goddard told me a story about a handicapped child from Easten, Maryland, who idolized Lefty. Goddard explained, "When I told Lefty about the boys problem, he immediately invited the youngster to his home. Once there, Lefty gave him a casting lesson and sent him home with a new Sage rod and reel as a gift."

I asked Ev, "What do you think Lefty would most like to be remembered for?" Her spontaneous reply, "He loves people." When I asked Lefty the same question, he was speechless. I thought about it for a day, and then it dawned on me that Lefty is so unpretentious that he has probably never given his own accomplishments much thought.

Lefty's friend, the recognized author and casting expert Ed Jaworowski, shared a statement made by Flip Pallot, star of ESPN's "Walkers Cay Chronicles". Everyone knows that Lefty holds angling legend, the late Joe Brooks, in the highest esteem. Joe was like a father to him. "Lefty is unaware of how far he has single handedly pushed this sport, even surpassing all that Joe did. But Lefty would be the last person to agree," Flip commented.

Bernard "Lefty" Kreh is as gracious a human being as God has put on the face of this Earth. I owe him a debt of gratitude for his guidance with my own writing and the consideration and encouragement he has given me over the past eight years. If you ever have the chance to attend one of his casting clinics, jump at the opportunity and treasure every moment. I promise you engaging conversation, lively entertainment and some of the best instruction you will ever get.

Chapter Ten

For The Road

Whether we visit the neighborhood pond, the babbling brook, or the open seas, the message of the water is the same: Be prepared, be patient, and enjoy the moment. Some days the fish will bite, some days they won't. In the grand scheme, the size of a day's catch isn't very important. But whenever we go down to the water and rediscover an important lesson about life — sure enough, that's a keeper.

– Criswell Freeman

The day before you leave on your fishing trip, contact the local fly fishing shop or guide service or the closest fish and game commission office to check conditions on the stretch of water where you will be fishing. The United States Geological Survey has up-to-date reports available for most streams and rivers throughout the country. They can be reached by phoning 1 (800) 872-6277 weekdays, or you can reach them on the Internet at http://www.water.usgs.gov/swt/.

It wouldn't hurt to confirm your room reservations, too!

The Information Super Highway

The Internet has rapidly become an important source of pertinent and timely information regarding all facets of our sport (Figure 10.1). *Fly Fisherman* Magazine's virtual fly shop home page, at http://www.flyshop.com is filled with interesting articles and the chat room is a valuable place to ask questions and share knowledge with other anglers. Other excellent web sites are, Flyfishing.com at http://www.flyfishing.com; FlyAngler's Online at http://www.flyanglersonline.com; and one of the best, Lefty's World at http://www.outdoors.net/lefty/.

Make Reservations Early

If you plan to stay overnight, make reservations and get a confirma-

Fly Fishing

TACKLE MANUFACTURERS

Internet Addresses

ABEL	http://www.Abelreels.com
ANDROS REELS	http://www.eliteflyfish.com
AYR REELS	http://www.ayr.com
CORTLAND	http://www.cortlandline.com
DIAMONDBACK RODS	http://www.cortlandline.com
FLYLOGIC	http://www.flylogic.com
G.LOOMIS	http://www.gloomis.com
HARDY	http://www.hardyusa.com
HEXAGRAPH RODS	http://www.hexagraph.com
J.A.FORBES LTD.	http://www.jaustinforbes.com
LAMSON	http://www.SAGEflyfish.com
MARRYAT	http://www.marryat.com
ORVIS	http://www.orvis.com
POWELL RODS	http://www.powellco.com
RAVEN RODS	http://www.RavenRod.com
REDINGTON	http://www.redington.com
ROSS REELS	http://www.ross-reels.com
ROYAL WULFF PRODUCTS	http://www.royalwulff.com
SAGE	http://www.SAGEflyfish.com
SCIENTIFIC ANGLERS	http://www.mmm.com/sciangler
SCOTT	http://www.scottflyrod.com
ST. CROIX RODS	http://www.stcroixrods.com
STH REELS	http://www.sthreels.com
THOMAS & THOMAS	http://www.thomasandthomas.com
WINSTON	http://www.winstonrods.com

FIGURE 10.1

tion number in advance. If a confirmation number is not available, at least write down the name of the person with whom you spoke, including the date and time in order to reconfirm that conversation upon your arrival. Doing so may save you the aggravation of having no room when you arrive. In regard to trips to another state, or out of the country, you may find it helpful to contact your local fly shop owner or the Federation of Fly Fishers or Trout Unlimited offices. More often than not, they have travel experience, or can at least refer you to a reputable travel agent or fishing lodge that does.

Better Safe Than Sorry

After check-in, store all the items that you will not need that day in your room and make sure the door is locked. Put your valuables in the hotel safe or lock them in your glove compartment. Do not leave expensive tackle, valuables or money in your room when you are not there. Put your car keys in a safe place, too, and always give a spare set to one of your fishing companions. Don't forget to check your cooler, if you brought one, to see if you need ice.

When you are done fishing for the day, make sure you collect all your gear streamside, and once back at your hotel, take an inventory of everything and store it in your room where it can be locked up safely for the night. If you can't park directly in front of your hotel room, do not leave money, valuables or tackle in your car overnight. Most reputable establishments carry insurance that covers fire and theft. In the latter case, don't forget to file a police report and check your homeowner's policy, too.

Don't Forget The Kids

One of the worst things you can do is push your child into the sport before he or she is ready. In such a case, the youngster will be difficult to teach at best, or worse will be completely turned off. Maturity and the desire to learn to fly fish varies with the individual child, and I do not feel kids can ever be too young to be taken along. However, it has been my experience that age ten seems to be a good time to start teaching children to fly fish. By that time they usually have enough physical strength and attention span to learn the basic skills, but remember to keep practice time to a minimum and your expectations realistic. For example, a ten-year-old should be able to tie a clinch knot, a double surgeon's knot and know how to do a side arm or a pick-up and lay-down cast.

The easiest way for a child to learn to cast is to have them stand safely and comfortably on the bank or in the water a few feet from the bank, facing upstream. Right handed children should cast from the left side of the stream and vice versa. It's important to have them tie on a fly that they'll be able to see or feel with ease. Twenty feet or so of fly line is a manageable length for kids and the 7-foot leader should be tapered to a 3X tippet. Instruct your child to hold the line securely against the grip in his or her rod hand for balance, and do a side-arm or a pick-up and lay-down upstream cast. This technique will help them keep their balance on the forward stroke. Once the fly floats or drifts past them and the line straightens out, simply have them lift the rod and cast upstream again, all in one motion. If they don't get a strike after a dozen or so attempts, have them walk or carefully wade ten or fifteen feet upstream and start casting again. By the way, it is a good idea to take your kids to a stream or pond where they are sure to catch fish. Nothing builds interest, enthusiasm and confidence faster!

The Federation of Fly Fishers, Trout Unlimited, some Girl Scout and Boy Scout troops, the YMCA and YWCA, as well as your local fly fishing shop sponsor "Kids Days" throughout the year. These programs are a great way to introduce your child to the sport because they are conducted by professionals, the locations are usually convenient and the cost, if any, is minimal.

Remember that every trip you take with your children builds memories that will last a lifetime. They will be listening and watching everything you say and do. As a result, your kids will learn a whole lot more than how to catch fish. By your example, they will learn your values concerning environmental and conservation issues, streamside etiquette, catch and release and life itself. They will see firsthand how you deal with success and failure. Teaching children is an awesome responsibility because in them lies the future of our sport.

MEDICAL EMERGENCIES

Some remote areas of the country may not have a healthcare facility close by, so it is imperative to bring a first aid kit and know how to use it. In addition, it is a good idea to fish with a friend for companionship, to share driving responsibility, and to have someone along who could provide assistance or go for help in the case of an emergency.

Water and graphite conduct electricity very well. Therefore, at the first sign of lightning, get out of the water and put your fly rod away. Either sit in your vehicle or get under a shelter, preferably indoors.

In regard to healthcare issues, never walk around camp barefoot. If you are bitten by a wild animal or snake, do not panic. Treat the wound with an antiseptic, apply a tourniquet if necessary or a sterile bandage and go to the nearest emergency room or doctor's office immediately.

It is easy to become preoccupied when fishing, even to the point of dehydration or exhaustion. The symptoms of heat exhaustion are weakness, nausea, dizziness, and profuse sweating, all of which result from physical exertion in the heat. If you experience any of these symptoms, sit down, preferably in the shade, bend over and place your head between your legs until you feel better. If the symptoms persist, go to a local healthcare facility. In all the excitement of your day on stream, do not forget to drink plenty of fluids, especially water. Also, remember to take your prescription medications, if needed, at the appropriate times. Insect bites and stings can be treated onsite from a first aid kit. Remember to bring directions to, and phone numbers for, the closest hospital, healthcare facility, doctor, or as a last resort a local veterinarian. This information can be obtained by a simple phone call to your destination's local flyfishing shop, outfitter's or chamber of commerce before you leave home. By the way, the chamber is an excellent source of sightseeing and other tourist information.

It is well documented that perfumes and heavy deodorants tend to attract annoying insects. Some suntan lotions and most insect repellents can actually destroy the finish on a fly line or rod when transferred during handling, so be careful when using these products. If you are fair-skinned, you will need a sun block and a long sleeve shirt. Suntan lotion should be applied twice, once after you shower and again before you go out to fish. Remember to smooth it on, don't rub it in. A hat with a bill or wide brim will protect your scalp, ears and eyes from the sun. Outdoor conditions everywhere can be very harsh, so you will also need excellent lip protection. This product can be purchased at your local ski shop, drugstore, or at some tackle dealers.

SKUNKED!

If you fish often enough, the day will come when nothing you try seems to work. Sooner or later everyone faces weather so inclement that it is virtually unfishable. On days like these, especially for the beginner, it is easy to become discouraged. The experienced angler, however, prepares himself or herself in advance for these challenges. Veterans bring those extras that turn unproductive time into constructive time. Think of these adversities as opportunities although there are some variables to consider. Are you fishing in or out of your home town, alone or with family or friends? Regardless of your circumstances, consider the following suggestions or, for that matter, be creative and make up your own!

You might: (1) reorganize your fly or tackle boxes; (2) clean and service your rods, reels and fly lines; (3) repair or replace your leaders; (4) tie some flies to replenish your stock; (5) repair the hole(s) in your leaky waders; (6) scout for some new streams; (7) visit a local fly shop, fishing personality or tourist attraction.

Please don't become disheartened. Before you give up on fishing entirely that day or pursue any of these suggestions, consider the fact that the bluewinged olive mayfly, for example, often hatch during bad weather, so look for them if it is not raining too hard. Remember, if the stream is muddy, you can still use a streamer, nymph or woolly bugger. If the fishing is really difficult and nothing seems to work, curl up with a good fishing book or watch a few angling videotapes until conditions improve.

W. WYNN

EPILOGUE

A WORD TO THE WISE

Don't be intimidated by things you may have read, written by well meaning 'experts'. Developing fly fishing skills is a learning process—start with the basics, and improvement will gradually come to those who are patient and willing to practice.

– *Leon Chandler*

To all fishermen, but especially to beginners, I say, "Please don't be too overwhelmed." Learning to fly fish takes time, and the rewards are well worth the effort. Newcomers take heart. As the late Odell Shepard wrote in his book, *Thy Rod and Thy Creel,* "In other arts and crafts, and even in a few sports, we can distinguish the three stages of apprentice, journeyman and master; but in angling few ever pass beyond apprenticeship, and masters there are none."

I understand the essence of what Odell Shepard meant. Fly fishing and all its associated skills can take a lifetime to develop. However, I consider professionals like Gary Borger, John Goddard, Lefty Kreh and Joan Wulff masters, yet each remains a student of the sport. You don't have to be an expert or fish *everyday* to enjoy it. I've taught hundreds of men and women who truly love to fly fish but aren't consumed by the sport.

Years ago, I mailed a survey to 36 of the preeminent fly fishing instructors in America. One of the questions I asked was, "What are the biggest problems facing beginners?" Many respondents agreed that most fly fishermen never attend a formal fly fishing school, and as a result don't give the finer points of the sport much thought. Yet study is one of the main ingredients for success.

When Lefty Kreh, editor Mac Seaholm and I discussed a title for this book, we agreed that it must include the words "trout" and "intelligent". According to Lefty, the reason for that decision was simple. "With all of the good information available today, including what's in this book, no intelligent trout fisherman should ever be unprepared for a day on stream."

You old-timers may have found a pearl of wisdom or two in this book, or enjoyed the anecdotes and biographies, but I challenge you to try something new and get out of that same old creek! For example, learn to cast with your opposite arm, explore a new trout stream or try out salmon, steelhead or saltwater fly fishing. Teach a kid to fish or volunteer your time to a local conservation organization. Your experience may be just what they need, and the self-satisfaction you receive can be rewarding beyond belief. Fly fishing is the experience of a lifetime, and a lifetime experience. The late angling legend, Theodore Gordon, acknowledged decades ago, "The great charm of fly-fishing is that we are always learning; no matter how long we have been at it, we are constantly making some fresh discovery." The day you stop learning is the day you stop growing. Keep alert and, above all, don't lose your patience, curiosity or your sense of humor.

Jerry McKinnis, that gracious and gentle angling personality who is the host of "The Fishin' Hole" on ESPN "Outdoors" once said during his show's introduction, "We don't walk on more common ground than when we fish." Trout don't discriminate, and to catch them on a fly is the ultimate one-on-one challenge. Prices for good tackle has become more reasonable, and there is excellent hands-on instruction available to more people now than ever before. Thanks to the hard work of groups like the Boy Scouts of America, Federation of Fly Fishers and Trout Unlimited many streams have become accessible to the handicapped, and I would encourage everyone to consider joining or contributing to any of the fine organizations that I've listed in the back of this book. Your donation of time, money or both will help preserve the sport for future generations.

Fly fishing is a great family pastime that offers adventure in some of the most beautiful locations throughout this country and the world.

Although I can't be there with you physically, as your instructor I am with you in spirit every day you log on stream. Always remember that fly fishing has a history, a tradition and a code of ethics. On behalf of all those visionary men and women who pioneered our sport, I welcome you to the fraternity.

Suggested Reading List

Our preoccupation with the nuts-and-bolts of fishing is shortsighted and shallow, and ignorance of a heritage that has persisted across five centuries of fly fishing literature is a shortcoming common to beginners and veterans alike. The sport is venerable and rich. It is unique, and it offers a remarkable palette of poetry.

– Ernest Schwiebert

A. Fly Patterns/Entomology
B. Literature
C. Instructional (Mechanics, techniques)
D. Humor/Philosophy/Personalities
E. History
F. Sciences
* Seminal and highly recommended

Most angling books will contain aspects of more than one of the above topics. I have attempted to group the titles into categories based on the major thrust of each work. Some of these titles may be out of print, but they are worth pursuing in angling shops or through new and used book dealers.

A. Fly Patterns and Entomology

Almy, Gerald. *Tying & Fishing Terrestrials.*
Stackpole, 1978. Harrisburg, Pa.

Bates, Joseph D. *Streamer Fly Tying and Fishing.*
Alfred Knopf, 1966. New York.

* Bergman, Ray. *Trout (Second Edition).*
Alfred A. Knopf, 1962. New York.

Borger, Gary. *Naturals.*
Stackpole, 1980. Harrisburg, Pa.

Borger, Gary. *Presentation.*
Tomorrow River Press, 1995. Wausau, Wi.

* Caucci, Al and Nastasi, Bob. *Hatches II.*
Nick Lyons Books/Lyons & Burford, Publishers, 1986. New York.

Koch, Ed. *Terrestrial Fishing.*
Stackpole, 1990. Harrisburg, Pa.

* LaFontaine, Gary. *Caddisflies.*
Nick Lyons Books/Winchester Press, 1981. New York.

Leonard, J. Edson. *Flies.*
A. S. Barnes & Co., Inc., 1988. New York.

Lively, Chauncy. *Chauncey Lively's Flybox.*
Stackpole Books, 1980. Harrisburg, Pa.

* McCafferty, W. Patrick. *Aquatic Entomology.*
Jones and Bartlett Publishers, 1981. Boston, London.

* McClane, A.J. (ed.). *McClane's New Standard Fishing*
Encyclopedia. Holt, Rinehart and Winston, 1972. New York.

McClane, A.J. *The Practical Fly Fisherman.*
Prentice-Hall, Inc., 1953. New Jersey.

* Marinaro, Vincent C. *A Modern Dry Fly Code.*
Alfred A. Knopf, 1972. New York.

Nemes, Sylvester. *The Soft-Hackled Fly.*
The Chatham Press, 1975. Old Greenwich.

* Proper, Datus. *What the Trout Said.*
Alfred Knopf, 1989. New York.

* Richards, Carl; Swisher, Doug; and Arbona, Fred. *Stoneflies.*
Nick Lyons Books/Winchester Press, 1980. New York.

* Whitlock, Dave. *Dave Whitlock's Guide to Aquatic Trout Foods.*
Nick Lyons Books/Winchester Press, 1982. New York.

B. Literature

* Gingrich, Arnold. *The Well-Tempered Angler.*
Alfred A. Knopf, 1965. New York.

Lamb, Dana S. *Bright Salmon and Brown Trout.*
Joh. Enschede'en Zonen, 1964. Holland.

Lamb, Dana S. *On Trout Streams and Salmon Rivers.*
Barre Publishers, 1963. Barre, Massachusetts.

Lamb, Dana S. *Where the Pools Are Bright and Deep.*
Winchester Press, 1973. New York.

McClane, A.J. (ed.). *McClane's New Standard Fishing*
Encyclopedia. Holt, Rinehart and Winston, 1972. New York.

McDonald, John. *The Origins of Angling.*
Doubleday & Co., Inc., 1963. Garden City, NY.

McDonald, John. *Quill Gordon.*
Nick Lyons Books/Winchester Press, 1972. New York.

Middleton, Harry. *The Starlight Creek Angling Society.*
Meadow Run Press, 1993. Stone Harbor, New Jersey.

Raines, Howell. *Fly Fishing Through The Midlife Crises.*
Bantam-Doubleday-Dell Publishing Group, Inc., 1993. New York.

Raymond, Steve. *The Year of the Angler.*
Winchester Press, 1973. New York.

Ritz, Charles. *A Fly Fisher's Life.*
Henry Holt & Co., 1972. New York.

Schullery, Paul. *American Fly Fishing.*
Nick Lyons Books, 1987. New York.

Schweibert, Ernest. *Remembrances of Rivers Past.*
MacMillan, 1972. New York.

Shepard, Odell. *Thy Rod & Thy Reel.*
Dodd, Mead & Co., 1930. New York.

Traver, Robert (AKA Voelker, John). *Anatomy of a Fisherman.*
McGraw-Hill, 1964. New York.

Traver, Robert (AKA Voelker, John). *Trout Madness.*
St. Martin's Press, 1960. New York.

Traver, Robert (AKA Voelker, John). *Trout Magic.*
Crown Publishers, 1974. New York.

Walden, Howard T. *Big Stony.*
The Derrydale Press, 1940. New York.

C. Instructional

Almy, Gerald. *Tying & Fishing Terrestrials.*
Stackpole, 1978. Harrisburg, Pa.

Bates, Joseph D. *Streamer Fly Tying and Fishing.*
Alfred Knopf, 1966. New York.

* Bergman, Ray. *Trout (Second Edition).*
Alfred A. Knopf, 1962. New York.

* Borger, Gary. *Naturals.*
Stackpole, 1980. Harrisburg, Pa.

* Borger, Gary. *Presentation.*
Tomorrow River Press, 1995. Wausau, Wi.

Brunquell, Philip M.D. *Fly-fishing with Children.*
The Countryman Press, 1994. Woodstock, Vermont.

* Caucci, Al and Nastasi, Bob. *Hatches II.*
Nick Lyons Books/Lyons & Burford, 1986. Publishers, New York.

* Goddard, John. *John Goddard's Trout-Fishing Techniques.*
Lyons & Burford Publishers, 1996. New York, New York.

Harvey, George. *Techniques of Fly Tying and Trout Fishing.*
Metz, 1985. Belleville.

* Jaworowski, Ed. *The Cast.*
Stockpole Books, 1992. Mechanicsburg, Pa.

Koch, Ed. *Terrestrial Fishing.*
Stackpole, 1990. Harrisburg, Pa.

* Kreh, Bernard "Lefty" and Sosin, Mark. *Practical Fishing Knots.*
Winchester Press, 1972. New Jersey.

Krieger, Mel. *The Essence of Flycasting.*
Club Pacific, 1987. San Francisco, Ca.

* LaFontaine, Gary. *Caddisflies.*
Nick Lyons Books/Winchester Press, 1981. New York.

Lee, Art. *Fishing Dry Flies for Trout on Rivers and Streams.*
Atheneum Publishers, Inc., 1982. New York.

Leonard, J. Edson. *Flies.*
A. S. Barnes & Co., Inc., 1950. New York.

* Marinaro, Vincent C. *A Modern Dry Fly Code.*
Alfred A. Knopf, 1972. New York.

McClane, A.J. (ed.). *McClane's New Standard Fishing Encyclopedia.* Holt, Rinehart and Winston, 1972. New York.

McClane, A.J. *The Practical Fly Fisherman.*
Prentice-Hall, Inc., 1953. New Jersey.

Meck, Charles and Hoover, Greg. *Great Rivers, Great Hatches*
Stackpole Books, 1992. Harrisburg, Pennsylvania.

* Merry, John A, *Best Fly Fishing Websites*
Specialized Marketing Agling, 1998. Cameron Park, California

Nemes, Sylvester. *The Soft-Hackled Fly.*
The Chatham Press, 1988. Old Greenwich.

* Proper, Datus. *What the Trout Said.*
Alfred Knopf, 1989. New York.

* Richards, Carl; Swisher, Doug; and Arbona, Fred. *Stoneflies.*
Nick Lyons Books/Winchester Press, 1980. New York.

Richards, Carl and Swisher, Doug. *Fly Fishing Strategy.*
Lyons & Burford Publishers, 1975. New York, New York.

Richards, Carl and Swisher, Doug. *Selective Trout.*
Lyons & Burford Publishers, 1986. New York, New York.

Ritz, Charles. *A Fly Fisher's Life.*
Henry Holt & Co., 1959. New York.

* Rosenbauer, Tom. *Prospecting for Trout.*
Delta Book. Bantam-Doubleday-Bell Publishing Group, Inc., 1993. New York.

* Rosenbauer, Tom. *Reading Trout Streams.*
The Lyons Press, 1988. New York.

* Rosenbauer, Tom. *The Orvis Fly Fishing Guide.*
Nick Lyons Books/Winchester Press, 1984. New York.

Schweibert, Ernest. *Nymphs.*
Winchester Press, 1973. New York.

Shaw-Kessler, Helen. *Flies for Fish and Fishermen.*
Stackpole Books, 1989. Harrisburg, PA.

Taller, Dick. *Fly Fishing for Trout.*
Lyons & Burford Publishers, 1974. New York, New York.

Wright, Leonard. *The Ways of Trout.*
Nick Lyons Books/Winchester, 1985. New York.

* Wulff, Joan. *Joan Wulff's Fly Casting Techniques.*
Lyons & Burford, 1987. New York, N.Y.

D. Humor, Philosophy and Personalities

Brunquell, Philip M.D. *Fly-fishing with Children.*
The Countryman Press, 1994. Woodstock, Vermont.

Genova, Phil. *First Cast.*
Stackpole Books, 1998. Mechanicsburg, Pennsylvania

* Gierach, John. *Trout Bum.*
Pruett Publishing Co., 1986. Boulder, Colorado.

* Gingrich, Arnold. *The Well-Tempered Angler.*
Alfred A. Knopf, 1973. New York.

* Gordon, Sid W. *How to Fish from Top to Bottom.*
The Stackpole Co., 1955. Harrisburg, Pa.

Henkin, Harmon. *Fly Tackle.*
J. B. Lippincott Company, 1976. New York.

Ritz, Charles. *A Fly Fisher's Life.*
Henry Holt & Co., 1959. New York.

Schullery, Paul. *American Fly Fishing.*
Nick Lyons Books, 1987. New York.

Traver, Robert (AKA Voelker, John). *Anatomy of a Fisherman.*
McGraw-Hill, 1964. New York.

Traver, Robert (AKA Voelker, John). *Trout Madness.*
St. Martin's Press, 1960. New York.

Traver, Robert (AKA Voelker, John). *Trout Magic.*
Crown Publishers, 1974. New York.

Walden, Howard T. *Big Stony.*
The Derrydale Press, 1940. New York.

White, Frederick. *The Spicklefisherman and Others.*
The Derrydale Press, 1928. New York.

Zern, Ed. and Webster, H.T. *To Hell with Fishing.*
D. Appelton-Century Co., Inc., 1945. New York.

Zern, Ed. *A Fine Kettle of Fish Stories.*
Winchester Press, 1973. New York.

E. History

Hills, John Waller. *A History of Fly Fishing.*
Freshet Press, 1921. New York.

McClane, A.J. (ed.). *McClane's New Standard Fishing Encyclopedia.* Holt, Rinehart and Winston, 1972. New York.

McDonald, John. *The Origins of Angling.*
Doubleday & Co., Inc., 1963. Garden City, NY.

McDonald, John. *Quill Gordon.*
Nick Lyons Books/Winchester Press, 1972. New York.

Merwin, John. *The New American Trout Fishing.*
Macmillan Publishing Company, 1994. New York.

Schullery, Paul. *American Fly Fishing.*
Nick Lyons Books, 1987. New York.

F. Sciences

Borger, Gary. *Naturals.*
Stackpole, 1980. Harrisburg, Pa.

* Caucci, Al and Nastasi, Bob. *Hatches II.*
Nick Lyons Books/Lyons & Burford, Publishers, 1986. New York.

* Gordon, Sid W. *How to Fish from Top to Bottom.*
The Stackpole Co., 1955. Harrisburg, Pa.

Needham, Paul R. *Trout Streams.*
Winchester Press, 1969. New York.

* McCafferty, W. Patrick. *Aquatic Entomology.*
Jones and Bartlett Publishers, 1981. Boston, London.

* McClane, A.J. (ed.). *McClane's New Standard Fishing*
Encyclopedia. Holt, Rinehart and Winston, 1972. New York.

* Sosin, Mark and Clark, John. *Through the Fish's Eye.*
Harper & Row, 1973. New York.

Sternberg, Dick. *Trout.*
Cy DeCasse Inc., 1996. Minnetonka, MN.

The Wildlife Series. *Trout.*
Stackpole Books, 1988. Mechanicsburg, PA.

* Whitlock, Dave. Dave Whitlock's Guide to Aquatic Trout Foods.
Nick Lyons Books/Winchester Press, 1982. New York.

* Willers, W.B. *Trout Biology.*
University of Wisconsin Press, 1981. Madison, WI.

Club and Conservation Organizations

American Museum of Fly-Fishing
Manchester, Vermont 05254

American Rivers Conservation Council
317 Pennsylvania Avenue S.E.
Washington, D. C. 20003

Atlantic Salmon Federation
1434 St. Catherine Street W.
Montreal, Quebec
Canada H3G 1R4

Big Hole River Foundation
P.O. Box 3894
Butte, Montana 59701

Boy Scouts of America
1325 W. Walnut Hill Lane
PO Box 152079
Irving, Texas 75038-2079

The Brotherhood of the Jungle Cock, Inc.
706 Orchard Way
Silver Spring, Maryland 20904-6232.25

Catskill Fly-Fishing Center & Museum
Old Route 17
Livingston Manor, New York 12758

Falling Springs Greenway, Inc.
P.O. Box 961
Chambersburg, PA 17201

The Federation of Fly Fishers
PO Box 1598
Bozeman, Montana 59771

Fly Fishers Club of Harrisburg
7 Oak Ridge Road
Carlise, Pennsylvania 17013

International Game Fish Association
3000 East Las Olas Boulevard
Fort Lauderdale, Florida 33316

Isaak Walton League
1800 North Kent Street, Suite 806
Arlington, Virginia 22209

Kettle Creek Watershed Association
c/o Amy Dubisz
RR #1, Box 184D
Covdersport, PA 16915

National Audubon Society
950 Third Avenue
New York, New York 10022

Pennsylvania Environmental
Defense Foundation
PO Box 371
Camp Hill, Pennsylvania 17001-0371

River Watch Network
153 State Street
Mt. Pelier, Vermont 05602

The Nature Conservancy
PO Box 258
Helena, Montana 59624

Trout Unlimited
1500 Wilson Blvd., Suite 310
Arlington, Virginia 22209

United Fishing Association, L.L.C.
925 Westchester Ave., 3rd Floor
White Plains, New York 10604

Yellow Breeches Anglers &
Conservation Association, Inc.
Box 1
Boiling Springs, PA 17001-0001

COLOPHON

This text has been typeset in 12.5 pt.
Goudy Old Style and printed by
Gilliland Printing
of Arkansas City, Kansas.
The paper is 60# white.

Index

A

B

C

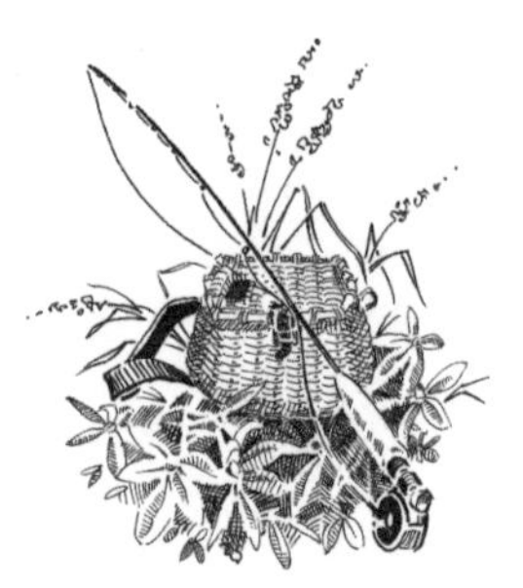